The Green Home Cleaning Guide: Clean Your House the Easy and Natural Way in Less than 30 Minutes a Day

by Michelle Anderson

This book contains material protected under International and Federal Copyright Laws and Treaties. Any unauthorized reprint or use of this material is prohibited. No part of this book may be reproduced or transmitted in any form or by any means, electronic or mechanical, including photocopying, recording, or by any information storage and retrieval system without express written permission from the author.

© 2013, Michael Anderson All rights reserved.

Disclaimer:

The information contained in this book is for general information purposes only. This book is sold with the understanding the author and/or publisher is not giving medical advice, nor should the information contained in this book replace medical advice, nor is it intended to diagnose or treat any disease, illness or other medical condition.

While we endeavor to keep the information up to date and correct, we make no representations or warranties of any kind, express or implied, about the completeness, accuracy, reliability, suitability or availability with respect to the book or the information, products, services, or related graphics contained book for any purpose. Any reliance you place on such information is therefore strictly at your own risk.

In no event will we be liable for any liability, loss or damage including without limitation, indirect or consequential loss or damage, or any loss or damage whatsoever arising from loss of data or profits arising out of, or in connection with, the use of the material or the interpretation of the material contained in this book.

Dedication:

This book is dedicated to my mother, the cleanest person I know. She managed to keep her home spotless and sparkling while raising no less than five rowdy and rambunctious kids, four of which were boys. A lot of the cleaning secrets I'm passing on in this book came from her.

Contents

1.0 Introduction 7
    A Bit About Me 13
    What This Book Is 15
    What This Book Isn't 16
2.0 The Basics 18
    Cleaning Special Surfaces 19
    Cleaning Blinds 22
    Supplies You'll Need 24
        A Mop and Bucket 24
        A Broom and Dustpan 26
        Microfiber Cloth 27
        Rubber Gloves 28
        Spray Bottles 29
        Sea Sponge 30
        Vacuum Cleaner 32
        Supply Caddy 33
        Scrub Brush 34
        Toilet Bowl Brush 35
    Elbow Grease 37

More Cleaner Doesn't Equal More Clean 39

3.0 Green Cleaners: Put the Harsh Chemicals Away ... 41

   Hydrogen Peroxide 42

      Uses for Peroxide 44

   White Vinegar 47

   Baking Soda: Not Just For Baking 52

   Lemon Juice 55

   Make Your Own Green Cleaning Products 58

      Dishwasher Detergent 60

      Dish Soap 60

      Natural Disinfectant 66

      Drain Cleaner 66

      Furniture Polish 67

      Homemade Laundry Detergent 69

      Oven Cleaner 72

      Toilet Bowl Cleaner 73

      Window and Glass Cleaner 74

4.0 The Clean Green Minimalism Cleaning Method: 4 Steps to Success 76

   Step 1: Commit to Keeping a Clean House 77

      How To Stop Procrastination Through Clean Green Thinking 79

   Step 2: Go Deep. 86

      What Is "Deep Cleaning?" 89

- Break It Down 90
- Top to Bottom Saves Time 93
- Set Up "Mess Blockers" To Save Time 95
- Deep Cleaning the Bathroom 97
- The Kitchen 108
- Living Room/Family Room 122
- Bedroom(s) 129
- The Laundry Room 134
- Outside 137
- The Garage 143
- Pat Yourself On the Back. 145

Step 3: Maintain. 146
- Tips To Help Keep the House Clean 149
- Put Your Family To Work 151
- Eliminate "Time Vampires" 153

Step 4: Spring Cleaning 160
- Clean Green Goodbye 161

1.0 Introduction

Minimalism.

Simplicity defined.

A minimalist seeks to live his or her life with only the items absolutely necessary to bring them happiness and joy.

A minimal lifestyle is a pipe dream for most of us. We have responsibilities and financial obligations preventing us from reaching a state of true minimalism—no matter how desirable it may sometimes seem.

What we can seek to do is implement minimalism in the areas of our lives where it will have the greatest impact. For most of us, one of those areas is cleaning. Instead of spending countless hours cleaning your home, minimalist cleaning allows you to keep your house clean in less than 30 minutes a day.

I know the deal.
Nobody ever plans on letting things get out of control.
You probably think about the mess around you constantly. After all, it's right there staring you in the face. Everywhere you look there's clutter.

You go to bed thinking about how you're going to attack the clutter and dirt and grime as soon as you get up. When you get up in the morning on the weekend, you start the day fully intending to clean all day and get things back under control.

Then life takes over.

One of your kids comes down with a nasty cold. Your significant other springs unannounced plans on you. Your son reminds you he has soccer practice for three hours smack dab in the middle of the day. There's an all-day marathon of your favorite show on TV and you decide to catch up on all the episodes you missed.

There's always something you can find to use as an excuse to avoid cleaning.

Instead of getting cleaner, your house gets messier and messier. The dishes begin to pile up. Your laundry room looks like a mountain range, with articles of clothing haphazardly thrown in ever-growing piles. You're having trouble seeing your countertops through all the bills, papers and assorted junk that's starting to pile up. You can write your name in the dust building up on top of the bookshelf.

I know how it is. I've been there.

There aren't enough hours in the day to keep things clean and finish everything else you need to do. I spent years trying to play catch-up with the mess in my house, constantly thinking there had to be a better way.

One day, I got fed up and decided to come up with a method to clean my house and keep it that way. I was tired of living in disarray and made my mind up to do something about it.

I didn't want to be a slave to my home, some sort of New-Age Cinderella doomed to cook and clean the entire day while my husband and children reaped the benefits of my labor. *I wanted a clean house, but not at the expense of every free second I had.*

I wanted to keep the house clean and still have time for myself.

"Impossible," you're saying. "That's not going to happen."

I thought so, too; until I started looking at the reasons cleaning was taking so much time. What I found was surprising. A good percentage of the time spent cleaning is wasted time; time that could be better spent doing other more enjoyable stuff.

There are time-suckers that can be eliminated from your daily routine that'll literally save you hours of time over the course of a week.

Just by eliminating these time-suckers, I was able to drastically reduce the time it took me to clean the house. We'll discuss these "time vampires" in a later section of the book. I'll tell you what they are and show you how to eliminate them.

Somewhere along the line during my transformation from messy mama to cleaning guru, I found minimalism. Not minimalism as in "live in a one-room hut in the woods and live with only 5 personal belongings" minimalism, which is the picture most people paint in their minds when they think of minimalism, but minimalism nonetheless. The minimalism I'm talking about is practiced in your home and requires a handful of changes that simplify your life.

My version of minimalism allows you to change your life for the positive with having to sell your personal belongings. Not that the purist view of minimalism isn't positive. I'm just not ready to go fully minimal. I enjoy TV and my computer and the occasional video game with my kids too much to give them up.

My brand of minimalism allows you to cut your cleaning time down to the bare minimum amount of time required to keep your house clean and free of clutter. I'd be lying to you if I told you it didn't require making changes in the way you live. Some of them are big changes; some of them are small. One thing's for certain. *They're all positive changes designed to help you lead a happier (and cleaner) life.*

You'll find yourself spending less time on the tasks you don't enjoy and more time on the stuff you do. In a nutshell, that's what minimalism is all about.

People tend to get stuck on the idea there's only one way to clean a house. After all, their mom did it that way...so did their grandmother...and their great grandmother...and so on and so on.

What you're about to learn is going to take a lot of what you thought you knew about cleaning and flip it on its head. Not only am I going to show you how to clean your house and keep it clean in the least amount of time possible, I'm going to show you how to do it GREEN.

That's right.

You're going to be able to clean faster and do it without having to breathe in the fumes of harsh chemicals.

You're only going to need a handful of items for your new green cleaning methods, most of which you probably already have in the house. If not, the items you're going to need can be purchased for pennies on the dollar when compared to the specialized cleaners most people are using.

It's going to take time to get used to the new method of cleaning your home. It's also going to take time to eliminate old ways of thinking. You've been programmed by the commercial cleaning industry to believe there's only one way to get stuff sparkly clean, and that's to use their expensive chemical products.

The truth is, there are products that are cheaper and more effective. Green products that, in some cases, have been in use for hundreds of years. Products that don't harm the environment because they're natural and break down into harmless substances found in nature.

The manufacturers of chemical cleaning products don't want the general population to know what I'm about to tell you. It would mean the end of the road for the poisons they're trying to push.

You're not going to need their chemical products by the time you're finished with this book.

I understand you're probably skeptical right now.

I was too.

Just do one thing for me. Enter this book with an open mind. Instead of dismissing the ideas and cleaning tools I introduce in later chapters without trying them, at least give them a fair shot before deciding they don't work.

If something doesn't work for you or doesn't fit into your lifestyle, don't do it. You don't have to do everything in this book to save time. Pick and choose the items you want to use. Feel free to adapt my techniques and the cleaners to suit your needs. I'm definitely not perfect and will be the first to admit there are tricks out there I haven't discovered yet.

I'm constantly finding new ways to speed up my daily tasks. I'm sure you will, too.

A Bit About Me

I've never been a big fan of books that start with a manifesto from the author detailing their entire life and all their accomplishments. The introduction more often than not amounts to nothing more than a chapter in which author brags and boasts about how much better he or she is than everyone else.

I debated whether or not to include this section. A lot, actually. I wrote an entire "About Me" section, then deleted it, then rewrote it a week later when I decided I should tell you a bit about myself lest you think I'm some sort of cleaning robot.

I'm a married mother. I have three children, two of which are like little tornadoes, running through the house misplacing everything they come in contact with. The two younger children are 3 years of age and 5 years of age. One boy and one girl, respectively.

The third child is a 12-year old girl. When it comes to cleaning, she's like a little angel sent down from the heavens above. Instead of creating messes, she usually helps clean them. It wasn't always that way, but recently she's really come into her own as a helper.

My husband plays both sides of the fence.

Some days he's helpful and picks up after himself. That's a rarity, and more often than not he's a completely different animal—one who leaves a trail of clothes and junk in his wake, seemingly disregarding every rule we've put in place to make cleaning simple and easy.

Our marriage is generally a good one—except on the days when he leaves the house in complete disarray. On those days, I want to kill him. Especially when he smiles at me and asks why I'm grouchy. He's lucky the domestic violence laws are pretty tough in the state in which we live.

You might be surprised to find I'm a little uncomfortable with the term "cleaning guru." I've been called a cleaning guru more than once and it always leaves me feeling a bit guilty.

I don't like it. Not one bit.

I'm really uncomfortable with it on the "cheat days" where I don't spend at least a little time cleaning my house. Yes, even my house gets messy from time-to-time.

Cleaning house is a war of attrition.

I'm of the opinion you're doing pretty good if your house is clean *most of the time*. Keeping it clean all the time is next to impossible.

What This Book Is

Figure 1: This book is designed to help you unchain yourself from your chores.

This book is a compilation of cleaning tips and tools designed to make life much easier on you. It introduces a method of cleaning created by me to make my life much easier. When I came up with this method, I had no plans of turning it into a book. I just wanted to make my life easier.

I've named this method of cleaning the **CGM (Clean Green Minimalism) Method**.

It's been designed with minimalism in mind. It's designed to cut down on the time required for cleaning, so you'll have more time to dedicate to other areas of your life.

It's designed to cut down on the cleaning tools and cleaners you'll need in an effort to make the CGM method of keeping your house clean as simple and easy to use as possible. It's also designed to be as easy on the environment as possible.

I've not only created a cleaning method that uses minimalism to simplify your cleaning tasks, I've used minimalism while writing and editing this book.

I've eliminated all but the most important stuff. I want it to be a quick read. You shouldn't have to slog through a thousand page manifesto to learn how to clean minimally.

What This Book Isn't

The Clean Green Minimalism (CGM) Method isn't a miracle cure for a dirty or cluttered home. You aren't going to snap your fingers and have a clean home without doing a thing. It's still going to take work and elbow grease to clean your home, especially if you've let things slide for a long period of time.

I've seen too many books and websites out there claiming to sell the "*Secrets to a Clean House.*" Some of them claim you can keep your house clean in just a few minutes a day. *This book isn't a miracle method that allows you to clean your house in minutes a day.*

I don't want to burst your bubble, but 5 minutes a day isn't going to cut it. Books that claim to allow you to keep your house clean in that short of a period of time are selling a pipe dream. For a normal sized house, a half hour a day is all you'll need, but only if you implement many of the techniques in this book.

The cleaning products I'm going to tell you about aren't miracle products.

I've seen products on the market claiming to be the greatest thing ever when it comes to cleaning tile . . . or hardwood floors . . . or windows . . . or . . . you get the point. I'm not going to tell you these products don't work. Some of them get the job done. The products in this book aren't miracle products that work a thousand times better than the chemicals you're currently using.

You aren't going to be able to spray them on and magically wipe away dirt and grime.

I will tell you this—I've yet to find a chemical product that works *better* than the household items I'm going to introduce to you in this book. I've found plenty that don't work as well.

This book isn't going to allow you to clean your house for free.

You're still going to have to buy products and cleaning tools to keep your house clean. The good news is the products I'm going to introduce you to are amongst the cheapest items you can buy when it comes to cleaning—and they're all green. There's no good reason not to use them, *unless you actually want to harm the environment*. If that's the case, put this book down and seek professional help.

Immediately.

Still with me? Good, let's get started.

2.0 The Basics

I'm going to make an assumption here that might appear a bit insulting at first. I'm going to assume you know nothing about cleaning and start from the basics.

I'm not making this assumption to insult you.

Some of my readers are going to need this section. **If you already know the basics of cleaning, you can skim this section and move on to the next one.**

The following indicator will be used to highlight important tips throughout the book. Whenever you see this banner, pay close attention because the information you're about to read is critical information.

IMPORTANT TIP

In an effort to keep things simple, this is the only banner I'm going to use. That way, when you see a banner, you'll know it's time to pay close attention.

Cleaning Special Surfaces

IMPORTANT TIP

Yes, we're staring the first section off with an important tip. I'm not going to waste your time here. This book is about minimal cleaning. I want to give you the most bang for your buck in the shortest amount of time possible.

This tip is one which might just save you more heartache and frustration than any other tip in the book. Not following this tip has the potential to ruin the item you're attempting to clean.
The cleaners in this book work well on most surfaces. Metal, glass, plastic, you name it; I've used the cleaners to clean them all. I've tested them on a number of surfaces and haven't found one in my household they can't safely and easily clean.

That doesn't mean they're safe for all surfaces.

Always, and I mean always, test new cleaners on a small (and preferably hidden) area of the item you're looking to clean. This will allow you to make sure the cleaner is compatible with the surface you're applying it to *before* you apply it to the entire surface.

Here's a fictionalized example of what can happen if you don't follow this advice:

Jane pays thousands of dollars for the latest and greatest in new countertops, the carbonized adamantium wood fiber counters (before you spend hours trying to look them up, let me tell you they don't exist). These new countertops are the latest and greatest in counters.

They're guaranteed to last forever and a year. The pamphlet that convinced Jane to buy them said they're basically impervious to everything. Jane didn't notice the small asterisk next to this statement or the even smaller print at the bottom laying out the few things these countertops *aren't* impervious to.

The small print on the documentation the counters came with states they're impervious to everything except for "Cleaner X." In fact, using this cleaner voids the warranty on these very expensive counters.

Jane didn't read the fine print (who does?) and doesn't follow the number one rule when it comes to using cleaning agents on a surface for the first time. Instead of applying the cleaner to a small out-of-sight area, she sprays it across the entire countertop and lets it sit for 30 seconds.

When she wipes it off, she finds the counters appear hazy and dull. Within days, the counters are peeling. She calls the warranty department, explains what happened and is told the damage won't be covered. Jane is devastated—and she's stuck with countertops she ruined because of her carelessness.

What can we learn from Jane?

While this is an extreme example, *it's an example of what can—and does—happen when you don't take the time to test a cleaner on a new surface before you start using it.*

Had Jane of tested her cleaner on a spot on the bottom of the counter near the back, she would have only had a small section of the counter with damage. And it would have been a section tucked away out of sight.

Always test your cleaners. If possible, test them on an area that's out of sight.

The cleaners in this book are safe on most surfaces. I've yet to see any damage from them on the surfaces I use them on daily. They're green cleaners and they're less harsh than most commercial cleaners. Just use a little common sense and test them first.

Cleaning Blinds

Figure 2: Most people turn a blind eye to their blinds.

There are a number of methods you can use to clean your blinds.

If they're just dusty, but don't have dirt and grime caked on them, you can simply dust them with a microfiber cloth. Try getting it damp to pick up even more dust.

For really dirty blinds (that aren't made of wood), take them down and bring them outside. Hang them over something and spray them down with the hose first, then clean them with distilled white vinegar. You can do this at home or take them to a self-service car wash so you can use the pressure hose.

IMPORTANT TIP

To speed up the process, get a pair of cotton gloves and put them on. Dip your fingers in distilled white vinegar and clean the blinds with the gloves while you're wearing them. The vinegar will help lift up stubborn dirt and grime.

Alternatively, you can use an old sock to do the same thing. Slip it over your hand and dip it in vinegar, then go to town.

IMPORTANT TIP

To speed the process up even more, take the blinds down and put them in the bathtub.

Fill the tub with warm water and add a couple cups of distilled white vinegar. Let them soak for an hour or two, wipe them down and rinse them off.

Supplies You'll Need

You aren't going to need to spend big bucks to fund your new CGM cleaning efforts. In fact, you've probably got everything you need. Well, everything except one or two ingredients for the recipes. We'll get to them in the next few chapters.

This section only covers the physical tools you need. Let's take a look at the tools you're going to want to make sure you have on hand.

A Mop and Bucket

Figure 3: Buy a good, old-fashioned mop and you'll be set.

A mop and a bucket are essential if you have tile, granite or hardwood floors.

There are a ton of mops available. Just a plain old string mop will do. No need to get too fancy. *I've bought a lot of different types of mops and have found the old-fashioned string mops work the best.*

You can use them for wet-mopping, damp-mopping and dry-mopping to good effect.

Wet-mopping is done by dipping the mop into the bucket, pulling it out and using the soaking wet mop on the surface you're cleaning. *Damp-mopping* takes place when you wring the mop out before using it on the floor. The mop is still damp, but not dripping water like it is during wet-mopping. *Dry-mopping* is, you guessed it, mopping with a completely dry mop. It's more like using a mop to dust the floors than it is mopping.

The bucket you choose is up to you. In a pinch, any bucket will do. If you want to get fancy, a wringer bucket will allow you to wring out the mop so you can more easily damp-mop a surface. This isn't a necessity, but can expand your cleaning options and speed things up if you plan on damp-mopping.

A Broom and Dustpan

Figure 4: Again, no need to get fancy.

A broom is the next tool you're going to need. A *bristle broom* can be used for all of your cleaning needs.

I use a bristle broom to sweep my kitchen and hallway. You can either get a straight-edge bristle broom or an angle broom. Once you get used to it, an angle broom allows you to make short work of corners, an area most brooms have trouble reaching into.

If you want to speed things up a bit, you're going to need a second type of broom.

A *push broom* is the second type of broom you're going to want. A push broom makes short work of larger areas like the garage, the patio and the driveway. If you don't already own one, you can buy a decent push broom for less than 20 bucks.

A dustpan will allow you to clean up the dirt and dust particles you've collected with the broom. Simply use the broom or a smaller brush to sweep the dirt onto the dustpan. You can stop sweeping it all under the fridge and start throwing it in the garbage.

Microfiber Cloth

Figure 5: The real quick picker-upper.

Microfiber cloth is a multipurpose cloth used for a number of tasks around the house. It's made of fine microfibers that are tightly woven together to create an efficient and powerful scrubbing tool that's durable and ultra-absorbent.

Microfiber cloth doesn't leave lint on the objects it comes in contact with. It's also better at picking up dirt and grime. You can use a microfiber cloth to dust your furniture, so you can throw that old duster you've been using away.

This type of cloth is marginally more expensive than regular cloth, but it works well enough to make the extra cash you'll spend well worth it. You can get 12 cloths for just over 10 bucks and they're re-washable, so the cost isn't all that prohibitive.

Rubber Gloves

Figure 6: Gloves protect the most important tool of all: your hands.

Rubber gloves will protect your hands when using cleaners. The cleaners we're going to be using aren't all that harsh, but it's still recommended you wear gloves. Even green cleaners can be tough on your skin, so make sure you wear your gloves whenever you're using any of the cleaners in this book.

Gloves can also be used to provide a barrier between your hands and the dirt and grime you're cleaning up. All kinds of bad stuff can build up when cleaning is ignored. Wear gloves to protect yourself from the harmful bacteria and microorganisms that may be sitting around your house.

Spray Bottles

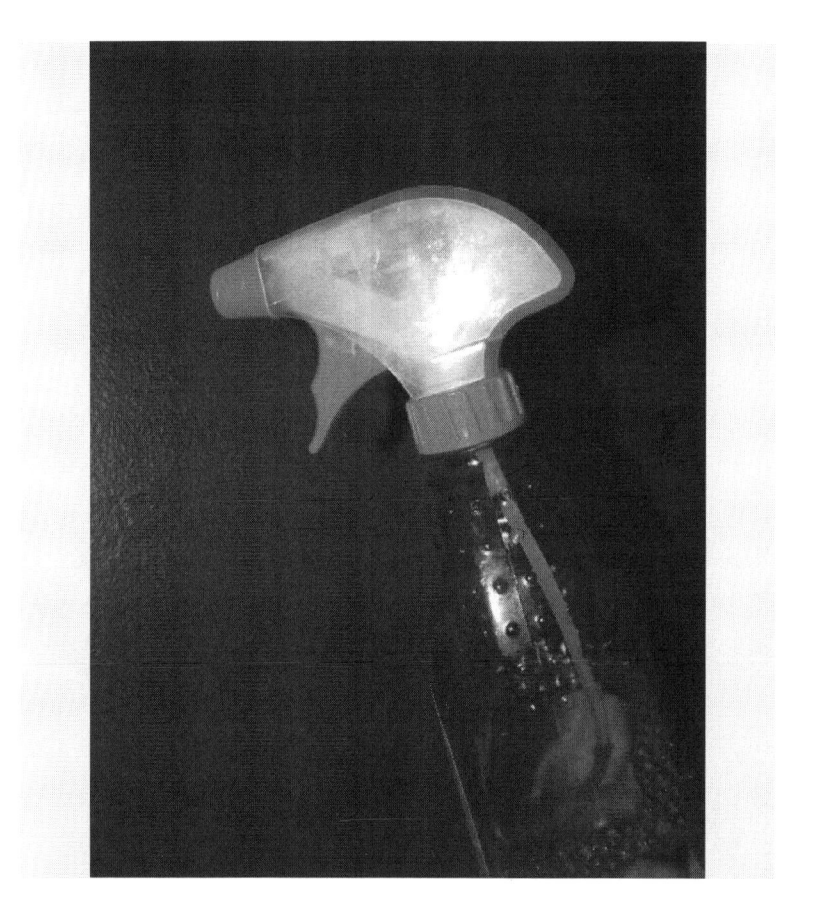

Figure 7: I wonder what's in this bottle.

Spray bottles make life much easier on you.
They can be used to store the cleaners you make and make it easy to disseminate cleaner across the surface you're cleaning. They also give you more control over how much cleaner you spraying on a surface.

IMPORTANT TIP

Make sure you label your spray bottles with whatever it is you put in them.

It may not seem like it at the time, but you aren't going to remember what's in a bottle a week or two down the road. Labeling your bottles makes it easy to find exactly what you need when you need it.

An unlabeled spray bottle is dangerous, as others who come across it won't know what's inside. While you'd like to think people wouldn't drink stuff out of an unlabeled spray bottle, it has happened and people have been poisoned because of it. The people who would drink out of an unlabeled spray bottle are probably the same type of people for which manufacturers have to label plastic bags as potential suffocation hazards.

Sea Sponge

Figure 8: Who lives in a pineapple under the sea?

If you don't understand the caption on the above image, ask any kid under the age of 12. Or any parent with kids under the age of 12.

There are two common types of sponges people use for cleaning: the sea sponge and the synthetic sponge. The *sea sponge* is a naturally growing sponge that can be sustainably grown and harvested. It contains natural enzymes that keep it free of bacteria and mildew for months on end.

The *synthetic sponge* is created in a factory using a process that's tough on the environment. Then it's dipped in *trisclosan*, a pesticide used to keep the sponge from becoming a giant colony of nasty microorganisms. They don't last as long as sea sponges and can't hold as much water.

I think the choice is pretty clear here: the synthetic sponge is the best choice.

Just kidding. I was checking to see if you're paying attention. **The sea sponge stands head and shoulders above synthetic sponges in every category that matters.** Go with a sea sponge and display it proudly.

Did I mention they look cool, too?

Vacuum Cleaner

Figure 9: Don't break the bank, but don't skimp too much either.

A vacuum cleaner is a must if you have carpets in your home. I'm not going to insult you by explaining what a vacuum cleaner is used for. I'm sure everyone at least knows what they're for.

IMPORTANT TIP

As soon as you can afford to, you owe it to yourself to invest in a good vacuum cleaner.

It doesn't have to be a $500 Dyson (although they do work great). Spend a couple hundred bucks and get a good vacuum and you'll be rewarded with a machine that picks stuff up the first time you go over it. Using a $50 Wally World special to vacuum your home is an exercise in frustration. You'll go over the same piece of lint a hundred times before the vacuum finally decides to pick it up.

Clean Green Minimalism requires that you clean your house in the most efficient manner possible. Running a vacuum over the same piece of lint 50 times will really slow you down. You won't be able to keep your home clean in 30 minutes a day if you spend 10 minutes on 1 small section of carpet.

Supply Caddy

What's the one item you can think of seeing every time you see a maid or a janitor in action?

That's right, a supply caddy or cart.

There's a good reason professional cleaners keep their supplies with them. Convenience.

Think how long it would take if a janitor had to walk all the way back to the janitor's closet every time he needed something. He might be able to clean one or two rooms a night. By carrying his supplies with him on a cart, the janitor has easy access to everything he needs. This allows him to save time and to finish as many rooms as he possibly can during his shift.

Now think of how much time you waste walking back and forth to your supplies.

You can do the same thing as the janitor, but on a smaller scale. You don't need a cart unless you have a huge mansion—and if you did, you wouldn't be reading this book. You'd be paying someone to do the cleaning for you. Someone with their own cart.

For those of us without the disposable income to hire help to do the cleaning, a supply caddy can really speed things up. Fill the caddy with the supplies you need and carry it with you from room to room. You'll find you save an amazing amount of time just by having the supplies you need on hand.

Scrub Brush

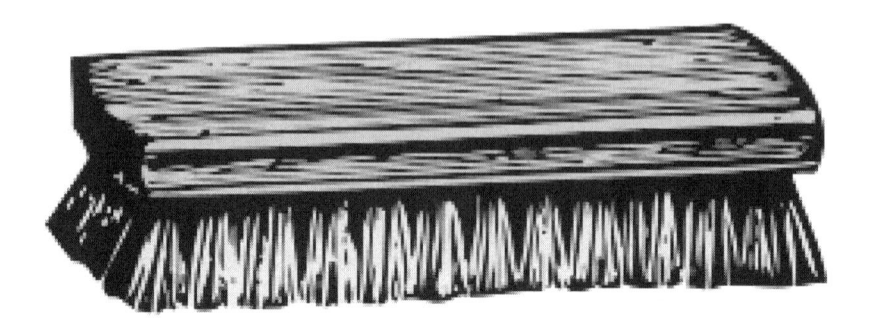

Figure 10: Scrub a dub dub.

A scrub brush is a good tool to have on hand. It can be used to clean grout and to scrub stubborn messes off a number of surfaces.

You can get scrub brushes with synthetic bristles or wire bristles. The *synthetic bristles* are good for jobs where there's a concern of scratching the surface you're cleaning. The *wire bristles* work best for tough jobs like cleaning baked on grime off of oven racks.

Toilet Bowl Brush

Figure 11: The majestic toilet brush.

This item will make life easier when cleaning the toilet. It allows you to clean all but the toughest of stains from your toilet without having to put your hands in the bowl.

If your husband is anything like mine, you don't want your hands anywhere near the bowl.

That's it. Those are the only items you need to keep your house clean.

Sure, there are items I'll mention later that you can use to make your life easier, but these items are the ones you absolutely need to own to implement the CGM method. The best part? You can buy all of the supplies (minus the good vacuum cleaner) for less than a hundred bucks total.

Go buy the items you don't have and come back. I'll wait right here.

Elbow Grease

Figure 12: Hope you've been working out!

There was one item I didn't mention in the previous section and that's elbow grease. If you've been putting off cleaning for a long time, you're going to need quite a bit of it.

It's going to take a bit of work to get things clean the first time around.

Make sure you use enough elbow grease to clean things right the first time through and it gets a lot easier the next time around. Doing a job halfway creates more work later on down the road. *Instead of adding more work later, why not do what it takes to get the job done right the first time around?*

That way, you'll have time to relax later. Time for yourself.

There's no way to avoid having to work while cleaning your home. Elbow grease is an essential part of cleaning. The only way to avoid it completely is to pay someone else to clean for you—and that gets expensive in a hurry.

Clean your home the right way and you'll minimize the amount of elbow grease you have to use every time you clean. Do things wrong and you're making a lot of work for yourself later on down the road.

IMPORTANT TIP

Thoroughly clean whatever it is you're cleaning each and every time you clean it.

Once an item or surface is clean, don't allow dirt and grime to build back up on it. *Taking the little bit of extra time it takes to clean something thoroughly each and every time you clean it will prevent a huge mess from building up.*

The microwave is a good example of something you should thoroughly clean after each use.

Keep a rag close by and wipe down any food that splatters while you're cooking. The food will be soft and pliable the first time around. If you give it time to build up, you're going to be looking at hours of work to clean something that would have took 30 seconds to wipe away if you cleaned it when it happened.

More Cleaner Doesn't Equal More Clean

Figure 13: Use only as much cleaner as you need.

Green cleaners are a good thing. They're better for the environment than chemical cleaners and do every bit as good of a job of cleaning.

The problem is, people have a tendency to use too much of a good thing. Just because it's a green cleansing agent doesn't mean you have to slather it on to get it to work. In fact, the opposite is usually the case. You only need a little bit to get things sparkling clean.

Using too much of any kind of cleaner makes it hard to remove that cleaner from the object you're cleaning. Residue will build up and the surface will actually become dirtier.

Here's why.

Soaps and cleaners contain agents that cause dirt to stick to them. When you use soap, the dirt sticks to the soap and is wiped away along with the soap when you clean the object off. Using too much soap makes it difficult to wipe away all the soap. Now, instead of having a clean surface which isn't likely to attract more dirt, you have a surface coated with a substance designed to attract dirt. See where this is headed?

The soap film you've left behind actually makes the object you've just cleaned get dirtier faster than it would have if you'd only used a small amount of soap.

How's that for fighting an uphill battle?

Use only as much cleaner or soap as you need in order to get a surface clean. Any more than that and you may be working against yourself.

3.0 Green Cleaning: Put the Harsh Chemicals Away

This section covers the *Green* in the Clean Green Minimalist Method of keeping a clean house. It gives you inexpensive green options for all the household cleaners you're going to need to keep your house clean.

There's a green alternative for pretty much any cleaner or soap you can think of. Chances are, there's more than one green option. To top it off, the replacements usually work as good or better—and they're cheaper—than the commercial products.

Excited yet? I've got more good news.

You can replace every commercial product you're currently using with only a handful of green alternatives. The best thing about green cleaners is they're multipurpose cleaners capable of a variety of cleaning tasks. You aren't going to need the specialty cleaners you've been using. All you're going to need are a few green alternatives designed to cover all bases.

Let's take a look at the cleaning products you need to have on hand.

Hydrogen Peroxide

Figure 14: Hydrogen Peroxide is the Swiss Army knife of green cleaners.

Hydrogen peroxide sounds like the name of a harsh chemical, but it isn't.

At the molecular level, it's simply a water molecule with an extra oxygen molecule added to it. It breaks down into oxygen and water. Plant and animal cells can form it naturally and it can be formed by light from the sun reacting with water.

You're probably already familiar hydrogen peroxide. It's the stuff you use to disinfect cuts that bubbles up when you dab it on a wound. *While disinfecting wounds and burns is the number one use for peroxide, it can be used for much, much more.*

Hydrogen peroxide is a more than capable replacement for chlorine bleach.

If bleach can do it, there's a pretty good chance hydrogen peroxide can do it too—and it's better for the environment. Chlorine bleach reacts with other elements in the environment to form toxic compounds. Hydrogen peroxide breaks down cleanly and doesn't form any toxic agents.

Hydrogen peroxide is such a good replacement for bleach, a number of companies that use bleach are making the switch to peroxide for industrial purposes. If manufacturers are willing to make the switch, it stands to reason it's a capable replacement for bleach at home.

IMPORTANT TIP

Peroxide comes in two forms: *food grade*, which is 35% peroxide and *3% peroxide*, which has been diluted to the point where it's safe for home use.

Never use food grade for home cleaning purposes.

It's corrosive and can make you sick if you ingest it or come in contact with it. 3% peroxide, on the other hand, is safe enough to use as mouthwash. Make sure you pay close attention to what you're buying.

3% peroxide can be purchased at most drugstores, pharmacies or department stores. There are people who purchase 35% peroxide and dilute it themselves. This is dangerous and I don't recommend it. 3% peroxide is inexpensive as it is. There's no need to handle a potentially harmful solution just save a few pennies.

Buy your peroxide by the gallon to save money.

It's good to have on hand and you'll use it long before it goes bad. It has a shelf life of more than six months once you've opened the bottle. It'll last even longer than that in a sealed bottle kept in a cool, dark place.

Store your peroxide out of direct sunlight.

It should be kept in a cool, dark place in a dark bottle. It will begin to break down rapidly if it's left in direct sunlight, or if it comes in contact with oxygen or water. A bottle that's left open will lose its potency in a matter of days, if not hours. A bottle that's been sealed back up tightly after use will last a hundred times that, if not longer.

Uses for Peroxide

Hydrogen peroxide isn't just a bleach replacement. It's like the Swiss Army Knife of green cleaners. I'm constantly experimenting and finding new uses for it.

Here's a list of the uses I've found thus far for peroxide:

- **Add 2 cups of hydrogen peroxide to a sink full of water and soak lace curtains in it for an hour to remove yellowing.** Rinse with cold water.
- **Add a capful of peroxide to the water when you water your plants to help prevent root rot.**

- **Add a tablespoon of hydrogen peroxide to a cup of water and use it as mouthwash or teeth whitener.** Don't swallow the solution. Make sure you rinse the remaining hydrogen peroxide from your mouth. The taste will take a little bit of getting used to.
- **After brushing your teeth, you can dip your toothbrush in hydrogen peroxide to clean it.** This will kill off microorganisms and bacteria that would otherwise thrive in your toothbrush.
- **Clean cutting boards with hydrogen peroxide to kill off salmonella.**
- **Clean your counters and tabletops with peroxide to disinfect them.**
- **Create a 1:5 solution of peroxide to water and use it to remove skunk smell.**
- **Create a 50/50 solution of hydrogen peroxide and water and add it to a spray bottle. Use it to clean your bathroom and toilet.** This solution is septic system friendly and is fine to use with grey water systems.
- **Keep fruit and vegetables fresher for longer and kill microorganisms and bacteria by adding a half cup of peroxide to a sink full of water and dipping your food in it.**
- **Make a paste with baking soda and use it to remove hard water stains.**
- **Mix hydrogen peroxide with baking soda to form a paste you can use as toothpaste.** As an added bonus, it whitens your teeth.

- **Mix two parts peroxide with one part water and use it as a spray to treat mold.** Make sure you properly dilute it if you plan on using it on painted areas, as it can cause the paint to fade.
- **Pour a capful of peroxide into your ear canal to clean it out.** The bubbles will tickle as it cleans out your ear.
- **Rub on bug bites, poison oak and poison ivy to stop the itching.**
- **Treat your carpet with it to remove urine stains and odors from your pets.** It will get the smell out and the pet won't be tempted to urinate there again.
- **Use hydrogen peroxide instead of bleach to wash your whites.** It's safe for your bright colors, too.
- **Use hydrogen peroxide to remove bloodstains.** Blot it on the stain and rinse it out immediately.
- **Use it to clean and disinfect minor cuts, bug bites and wounds.**
- **Use it to remove punch or red wine stains from fabric or carpet.**
- **Use it to treat toenail fungus.**
- **Use it with a microfiber cloth to clean mirrors and glass with no streaking.**

IMPORTANT TIP

All of the uses for peroxide in this book call for 3% peroxide. The tips that call for dilution of peroxide further dilute 3% peroxide.

White Vinegar

Figure 15: Distilled white vinegar is a green cleaner's best friend.

Distilled white vinegar is another green cleaner you should always have on hand.

White vinegar is in a three-way tie with baking soda and hydrogen peroxide as my favorite cleaner. It's every bit as effective as hydrogen peroxide for most of the home cleaning uses mentioned in the previous section. Just don't use it as mouthwash, toothpaste or put it on open wounds.

The acidity in distilled white vinegar makes it an effective cleaner that can be used for a large number of cleaning tasks, including the following:

- **Add it to baking soda to create a paste you can use as a scouring cleaner.** You can add a

tablespoon of dish soap to it to further enhance its cleaning capabilities. The vinegar and baking soda will quickly neutralize one another, so don't store this mixture. Mix it as you need it.
- **Use distilled white vinegar to remove mineral deposits from coffee makers.** It can also be used to remove stains from coffee cups.
- **It's great for removing hard water stains and lime build-up.**
- **Add a lemon and a cup of white vinegar to your drain and use the garbage disposal to chop up the lemon in order to clean and deodorize your drain.**
- **Use it to clean tarnished metals.**
- **Spray around areas where ants are entering the home to keep them out.**
- **Polish porcelain sinks with distilled white vinegar.**
- **Use as an all-purpose cleaner for your car.**
- **Use it to remove stains from your carpet.** The mixture has to be left on the carpet overnight, and then vacuumed up in the morning.
- **Use it to clean your grill.**
- **Use as a multipurpose cleaner.**
- **Clean grime, mildew and mold off of almost any surface.** It works great to clean bathrooms, kitchens and showers.
- **Use it to clean grout by spraying it onto the grout and letting it sit for five minutes before cleaning it off.**

- **Soothe sunburns, insect bites and bee stings by rubbing it on the affected area.**
- **Rub it on cuts, scrapes and burns to kill germs.**
- **Use it to make your whites whiter and your brights bolder by adding a cup to your laundry.** It can be used to remove perspiration stains, smoke odors and scorch marks from clothes.
- **Use it to clean soot from your fireplace.**
- **Here's an easy way to clean your blinds.** Get a pair of white cotton gloves and put them on. Dip the fingers in a 1:1 solution of distilled white vinegar and water and use the gloves to clean the blinds. Much easier than scrubbing with a rag!
- **Distilled white vinegar can be used to break down wallpaper glue and is a good sticker remover.**
- **Shine your shoes and polish leather with distilled white vinegar.**
- **Use it to shine vinyl or linoleum floors.**
- **Clean countertops and tile with a microfiber cloth soaked in distilled white vinegar.**
- **Use it to clean the toilet.** Dump a cup or two of distilled white vinegar into the toilet and let it sit overnight.
- **Use it to clear up clogged showerheads by placing it in a plastic bag and tying the plastic bag off so the showerhead is soaking in it.** Leave the bag in place for a couple hours.

- **Distilled white vinegar can be used as a degreaser.** Spray it on baked-on grease and let it sit for 20 minutes, then wipe it away.
- **Run a cupful through your dishwasher and washing machine on an empty cycle to clean out soap scum.**
- **Soak a paper towel in it and wrap it around glassware to remove cloudy build-up.**
- **White vinegar works great to remove odors.** Lunchboxes, fridges, drains…You name it, you can probably deodorize it with distilled white vinegar.
- **Use a 1:1 mixture of distilled white vinegar and water to clean your microwave and refrigerator.** When using it in the microwave, place a bowl of it in the microwave and bring it to a boil for a couple minutes to loosen stuck-on foods.
- **Clean wood paneling with a 1:3 solution of white vinegar to water.**
- **Create a paste using a 2:1 mixture of salt to vinegar and use it to polish chrome.**

IMPORTANT TIP

If you're in middle of cleaning and realize you don't have distilled white vinegar, you can substitute hydrogen peroxide for most of the cleaning tasks white vinegar is used for.

IMPORTANT TIP

Never use distilled white vinegar on marble. It can etch the surface and damage the marble. *This is one of the few surfaces distilled white vinegar can't safely clean.*

Baking Soda: Not Just For Baking

Baking soda come in handy in the kitchen, where it's used as a leavening agent. What most people don't realize is it can also be used to clean the kitchen once you're done cooking.

If you only have three natural cleaners, they better be baking soda, hydrogen peroxide and distilled white vinegar. There isn't much you can't clean if you have these handy green cleaners on hand.

Baking soda has the following household uses:

- **Add a couple tablespoons to a cup of water and use it to clean marble furniture.**
- **Add it to your toilet, wait an hour and scrub it out.** It will clean and deodorize your toilet.
- **Add it to your washing machine to help remove stains from dirty clothes.**
- **Add to bathwater in order to soften your skin.**
- **Add to the water in your flower vase to keep flowers fresher for longer.**
- **Apply it to your armpits and it acts as deodorant.**
- **Combine with bath salts in small netted bags to create a good-smelling air freshener.**
- **Dump half a box in the drain and let it sit for an hour, then wash it down to keep your drains clean.**

- Make a paste out of baking soda and water and use it to remove crayon marks from walls and floors.
- Mix with water and use as an all-purpose cleaner capable of cleaning most surfaces in your home.
- Put out minor wood and upholstery fires by sprinkling baking soda on them.
- Relieves diaper rash.
- Relieves insect stings and sunburn pain.
- Removes strong odors from almost anything. Sprinkle it on the affected area or set a box of baking soda in the area with the bad smell. Works great for eliminating bad smells from refrigerators.
- Sprinkle baking soda on your carpet and vacuum it up to keep your carpet clean and smelling fresh.
- Sprinkle it in areas where bugs are a problem to get rid of the bugs.
- Sprinkle it in your shoes to eliminate foot odor.
- Take it orally and it acts as an antacid.
- Use it as a denture cleaner.
- Use it to clean mirrors without streaking.
- Works well as a degreaser.

IMPORTANT TIP

There are a lot of home cleaning product recipes that call for mixing baking soda with vinegar. I've seen them in print and all over the Internet. The people who created these recipes must not have passed their fifth grade science class.

Baking soda is alkaline and vinegar is acidic, which means these two cleaners will react with one another and neutralize one another.

When you mix these two cleaners, you're not getting a cleaner that's twice as good; you're getting something similar to water. If you want to use vinegar and baking soda on a surface, use them separately.

If you don't believe me, try mixing the two in a cup and watch what happens. Don't stand too close, as the reaction will create a bubbling mess. That's the acid and base reacting to one another and cancelling each other out.

There is one good use for the mixture. Pour a cup of baking soda into a clogged drain and follow it up with a cup of distilled white vinegar. The reaction can sometimes loosen up the clog and clear the drain.

The only other good use for this mixture is to mix it up and immediately use it as an abrasive cleaner. The bubbles help lift gunk and grime off the surface they're attached to. As mentioned previously, don't let this mixture sit and don't try to store it already mixed. Mix it as you're using it for best effect.

Lemon Juice

Figure 16: Lemon juice - Not just for lemonade.

Lemon juice acts as a disinfectant and can be used as a natural cleaner that leaves everything you clean with it smelling great. It's not as ubiquitous as the other cleaners, but it has its place in the world of green cleaners.

The following items can be polished or cleaned with lemon juice:

- **Anything with hard water stains.**
- **Baked-on foods.** Microwave a cup containing equal parts water and lemon juice until it starts to

boil, then let it sit for 20 minutes. The previously baked-on foods should be able to be wiped away.
- **Chrome.**
- **Copper.**
- **Cutting boards.**
- **Food containers.**
- **Grates.**
- **Grills.**
- **Grout.**
- **Hardwood floors.**
- **Mirrors.**
- **Most woods.**
- **The toilet.**
- **Tile.**
- **Use it to remove grease.**
- **Use it to remove some stains from clothing by applying the juice directly to the stain.**
- **Windows.**
- **You.** Use it to clean your hair, your face and your body.
- **Your garbage disposal.**

IMPORTANT TIP

Keep lemon juice away from brass-plated objects because it will damage them upon contact. Brass-plated objects are one of the few surfaces you can't use lemon juice on.

Strangely enough, solid brass objects can be cleaned with lemon juice mixed with salt. Don't use a lemon juice cleaning solution on a brass object unless you're absolutely positive it's solid brass. Even then, test it in a small area first, just to be safe.

Make Your Own Green Cleaning Products

The following recipes will allow you to make your own "specialized" cleaners at home using all natural ingredients. Making your own green cleaners at home will allow you to save money while saving the environment.

The cleaners listed below are quick and easy to make. I've listed green commercial alternatives (when they're available) for those who don't have time to make their own cleaners.

These recipes call for a few items not mentioned in the previous section. Rest assured all of the items called for in these recipes are considered green and all-natural. The ingredients are available in most grocery or drugstores and best of all, they're cheap. It costs significantly less to make your own products than it does to buy them already made.

Here are the ingredients you're going to need:

- **Baking soda.**
- **Borax**: This is a naturally occurring ingredient that can also be created in a laboratory setting. Most stores that carry laundry detergent carry Borax in the same section. 20-Mule Team Borax is a popular brand.
- **Citric acid**: Made from citrus fruits. Use food-grade citric acid.
- **Essential oils**: These helpful oils are made of the aromatic essence of plants. They're used to add

scent to homemade products and to give some products a little extra boost.
- **Hydrogen peroxide.**
- **Kosher salt**: Pure salt.
- **Lemon juice.**
- **Liquid castile soap**: This soap is made from olive oil and breaks down into natural compounds.
- **Washing Soda (Sodium Carbonate)**: This is a strong degreaser made from salt and limestone. It's available in some drug and grocery stores. If you can't find it, you can buy it online.
- **White vinegar.**

Gather all the ingredients, along with some bottles to store them in. You're going to want some of these homemade natural cleaning products on hand. Take an hour or two and mix up the ones you're going to need in advance. This step alone will save you a lot of time during your daily cleaning sessions.

All-Purpose Cleaner

This all-purpose cleaner is designed to be used for, well, all purposes. Use microfiber cloth with this cleaner for best results.

Here are the ingredients you're going to need:

- ½ cup vinegar
- 3 teaspoons Borax
- 5 cups water.

Mix well and add the mixture to a spray bottle. This cleaner works well for most purposes and you should always have a batch at the ready. If this cleaner doesn't get the job done, you may have to whip up a batch of one of the other recipes in this chapter.

Green commercial products include the following:

- Simple Green All-Purpose Cleaner.
- Green Works All-Purpose Cleaner.
- Misty Green All-Purpose Cleaner.

Air Freshener

There are a number of natural items you can use as air fresheners.

The easiest is probably a box of baking soda. All you have to do is open up the box and leave it sitting in the area you want to deodorize. For larger rooms you might need more than one box.

Baking soda works great to deodorize refrigerators. Just don't use the baking soda for cooking after using it as an air freshener. It will impart all sorts of smells and tastes into the dish you're cooking.

Fresh coffee grounds are another good choice. Grind up a cup of coffee beans and spread them out in a small dish. The more coffee grounds you have spread out, the more powerful of an air freshener you're going to have.

You can also freshen the air with essential oil blends.

Buy a variety of essential oils and mix and match them to your heart's delight. You can make interesting smelling blends and diffuse them into a room with a diffuser, which is an item designed to slowly release the scent of the oil blend into your room.

Dish Soap

Combine the following ingredients to make your own dish soap at home:

- ➢ 1 cup water
- ➢ 10 drops lemon essential oil
- ➢ 3 cups liquid castile soap

This soap is intended to be used in the same manner you'd use dish soap. It shouldn't be used in your dishwasher unless you want a house full of foam. You can substitute the lemon essential oil for any essential oil you like. Other favorites of mine include lavender and orange essential oils.

The following products are commercial green dish soaps:

- ➢ BioKleen Dishwashing Liquid.
- ➢ 7th Generation Natural Dishwashing Liquid.
- ➢ LifeTree Home Soap.
- ➢ Method Dish Soap.

IMPORTANT TIP

If you find this formula isn't cutting it when it comes to getting rid of heavy grease on your dishes, add a 1/2 cup of lemon juice to the dishwater in your sink while you're doing the dishes.

Whatever you do, don't add it directly to the dish soap. It will cause the soap to curdle and go bad.

If you find your dishes are spotting, try adding a half cup of white vinegar to the dishwater. Again, don't add it directly to the soap and store it that way. It should be added to the dishwater while you're doing the dishes.

Dishwasher Detergent

This all-natural detergent makes short work of greasy dishes. For best results, add distilled white vinegar to the rinse reservoir when using this detergent.

Mix the following ingredients together:

- 2 cups Borax
- 2 cups washing soda
- 1 cup Kosher salt
- 1 cup citric acid

Mix thoroughly and store in an airtight container. Use a single tablespoon of this mixture per load of dishes.

Alternatively, you can buy the following green products:

- Biokleen Dish Powder.
- CitraDish Automatic Dishwashing Detergent.
- Method Smarty Dish Detergent.
- Ecover Dishwasher Tablets.
- 7th Generation Automatic Dishwashing Gel or Powder.

The commercial green products will run you between $0.20 and $0.50 a load. Making your own costs somewhere in the range of $0.08 to $0.12 a load.

IMPORTANT TIP

If you're finding your dishes have a milky film on them after using this detergent, add a capful of liquid dish soap to the mixture. This will eliminate the film.

Drain Cleaner

Have you ever seen the volcano science fair experiments where kids build an erupting volcano? This is the mixture they use to make it "erupt." The reaction between the baking soda and vinegar in your drain is usually enough to dislodge any clogs.

Dump half a box of baking soda down the drain and let it sit for 5 minutes. Follow that up with a cup of distilled white vinegar.

The following green drain cleaners are available commercially:

- BioKleen BacOut.
- Earth Friendly Enzymatic Drain Cleaner.

IMPORTANT TIP

If baking soda and vinegar alone isn't enough to clear the drain, wait 15 minutes and pour a pot of boiling water down the drain. This will melt the built-up grease and should clear the clog. Don't use this method if you have plastic pipes, as it can damage the pipes.

Furniture Polish

Mix 6 drops lemon essential oil into a cup of warm water. Shake up and spray onto a damp microfiber cloth. Wipe onto the surface you're trying to polish and wipe away with a dry cloth.

Alternatively, you can pay a lot more for the following commercial products:

- Earth Friendly Furniture Polish.
- Simple Green Streak-Free Polish.

Gum Remover

There are two methods you can use to remove gum from fabric, furniture, your carpet or your clothes. These methods will also work to remove gum that's stuck in your kid's hair. No more cutting out huge chunks of hair and hoping no one notices!

In order to remove gum, you're going to need two items most people already have in their home:

- Creamy peanut butter.
- Ice.

First, take the ice and rub it on the gum for a couple minutes until it starts to get hard. Alternatively, if you're dealing with something small like an article of clothing, you can toss it in the freezer.

Once the gum hardens up, break it up and remove it.

If there are any stubborn pieces you can't get out with ice, you may have to take a more drastic measure. Let the gum soften back up and apply peanut butter to it. Rub the peanut butter into the gum and use a moist cloth to wipe it away. This should lift the gum out of the fabric or whatever it's stuck in.

There's just one problem. You now have peanut oil to deal with. Don't worry—it's a lot easier to remove than the gum. A damp cloth with a bit of baking soda added to it should be able to make short work of the peanut oil and you'll be left with an item that's free of gum.

Homemade Laundry Detergent

When I first decided to make laundry detergent at home, most of the recipes I found created less-than-satisfactory detergents that I wasn't happy with. I played around with the mixtures and came up with this one that works every bit as good as the stuff sold in the stores.

The best part?

It only requires a handful of ingredients and works in high-efficiency washers. You only need a tablespoon or two of this stuff to clean an entire load of laundry.

Here are the ingredients you need for this recipe:

- 1 bar of castile soap
- 1 cup of washing soda
- 1 cup of Borax

Follow these instructions to make your laundry soap:

1. Shave the bar of soap into fine shavings. I use a cheese grater and shave it with the smallest holes on the grater. Alternatively, you can grind up small amounts in your blender. You want the soap to be ground to as fine of a powder as you can get it.
2. Add the borax and the washing soda to the mix.
3. Stir it up until it you have a fine powder.

The following green commercial products are available:

- 7th Generation Green Detergent.

- Rockin' Green Laundry Detergent.
- Green Works Natural Laundry Detergent.
- Mrs. Meyers Clean Day.
- Arm & Hammer Essentials Liquid Laundry Detergent.
- Country Save Laundry Detergent.

IMPORTANT TIP

Add half a cup of vinegar to each load of laundry to get rid of any residue left behind by the soap.

Natural Disinfectant

Mix the following ingredients:

- 5 tablespoon distilled white vinegar
- 3 teaspoons Borax
- 1/2 teaspoon liquid castile soap
- 3 cups hot water
- 10 drops of the essential oil(s) of your choice

Spray the disinfectant on the surface you wish to disinfect and wipe it off with a microfiber cloth. You can also use this formula to clean and disinfect old sponges by dipping them in it and letting them soak up the mixture.

The following products are commercially-sold green disinfectants:

- Simple Green One-Step Disinfectant.
- CleanDegrees Green Disinfectant.
- PureGreen 24 Disinfectant.

Oven Cleaner

Mix the following ingredients together until they become a paste:

- ➢ 1 cup baking soda
- ➢ 1/4 cup water
- ➢ 1/4 cup Kosher salt

Apply the paste to the interior of the oven and let sit for six to 12 hours, then wipe away. Steel wool can be used on troublesome areas.

Arm & Hammer Oven Cleaner is the best green commercial alternative.

Toilet Bowl Cleaner

Pour a half cup baking soda and a 1/2 cup of Borax into the toilet and let sit for a couple hours. Scrub with a toilet brush and flush.

Alternatively, you can pour straight white vinegar into the toilet and leave it there for an hour.

Or you can pour straight baking soda in and let it sit.

Yet another option is to mix 2 parts Borax to 1 part lemon juice and apply it to the toilet as a paste. Let it sit for 3 hours and scrub it off.

Green commercial products include:

- Green Works Natural Toilet Cleaner.
- 7th Generation Toilet Bowl Cleaner.

IMPORTANT TIP

Hard water can leave stubborn stains that no cleaner, commercial or homemade, is able to remove on its own. Get a pumice stone and rub the stains gently to remove them.

Window and Glass Cleaner

Mix 2 teaspoons of white vinegar into 3 cups of water and spray on the surface you wish to clean.

Wipe away with a clean microfiber cloth.

Be careful not to use too much vinegar and don't apply to windows that have been heated by the sun or you run the risk of clouding the glass.

Citraclear Window and Glass Cleaner is a green commercial window cleaner you can use if you don't feel like making your own.

Wood Floor Cleaner

Wood floors are centerpiece of many homes. They look great and add a touch of class to almost any house they're installed in.

Cleaning wood floors is easy. All-natural wood floor cleaner only requires 2 ingredients:

- ➢ White vinegar
- ➢ A bucket of arm water

Pour two cups of white vinegar into the bucket of warm water. Damp-mop the floor with this mixture and let it air-dry. You can swap out the white vinegar for lemon juice if you want the room you're mopping to have a fresh lemon scent.

4.0 The Clean Green Minimalism Cleaning Method: 4 Steps to Success

Here's the deal. All it's going to take is 4 simple steps to get your house clean and keep it that way. These steps are simple, but don't be fooled into thinking that means they're going to be easy, especially at first. It gets easier later on down the road, but you're going to have to be willing to work hard for now.

The good news is the hardest steps are the first two and you only have to do them once if you play your cards right. *Once you're past the first two steps, keeping your home clean is simply a matter of cycling through steps 3 through 5 in a continuous cycle.*

This is the most important section of the book. It lays out the system you need to use to keep your house clean *the easy way*. It's still going to take work, but nowhere near as much work as it would normally take.

Step 1: Commit to Keeping a Clean House.

The CGM Method isn't a miracle cure for your house-cleaning woes. There isn't a house-cleaning fairy that's going to fly into your house once a day and clean your house for you. Even if there was, I wouldn't tell you how to call her.

I'd be using her for my house.

To get and keep your house clean, it's going to take commitment.

You have to make the decision right now that you're tired of living in a messy home and you're going to do something about. If you're sitting in your house reading this book, take a good look around you. If you're somewhere else, close your eyes and picture the messiest area of your home.

How does it make you feel?

Guilty?

Sad?

Angry because you let things get to this point?

Frustrated that you haven't kept up on things like you know you should have?

A dirty home works against you on multiple levels. You start off irritated about the mess, but let it go because you have better things to do. This minor mess slowly grows into a bigger mess that starts to really bother you. You're bothered by the bigger mess, but feel you don't have time to clean it up because there's always something else that seems more important that needs to be done.

Maybe you start cleaning, only to get frustrated at the fact you don't seem to be making any leeway. This can lead to feelings of sadness, anger, depression and even despair as the mess spirals out of control.

Your home is supposed to be your sanctuary—a place in which you can relax and feel good about yourself.

Those with large families are probably laughing to themselves right now. Relax? Yeah, right. Relaxation is relative. You should, at the very least, be able to feel comfortable in your home and looking around your house shouldn't evoke negative feelings. Being at home should be a positive experience. It's difficult to obtain that level of comfort in a house that's a mess.

You can keep your house clean.

Millions of people around the globe do it. Some with larger families than yours.

You just have to commit to it.

Get motivated and get to cleaning.

How To Stop Procrastination Through Clean Green Thinking

I'll do it later.
I need to finish this task, but I just don't have time.
I know I should be cleaning right now.
I have to do this task.
I should have already cleaned the entire house.
I need to clean.

All of the thoughts above are used by procrastinators to put off the cleaning tasks they should be doing.

I like to call thoughts like the ones above *procrastination triggers*. They're the thoughts that allow us to put off cleaning until another time—a time that never comes because when it does, another procrastination trigger allows us to put off cleaning once again.

I call this process of procrastination a *procrastination cycle*. Here's a picture showing the procrastination cycle in action:

```
        THINK ABOUT
         CLEANING

LOSE DESIRE          PROCRASTINATION
 TO CLEAN                TRIGGER
```

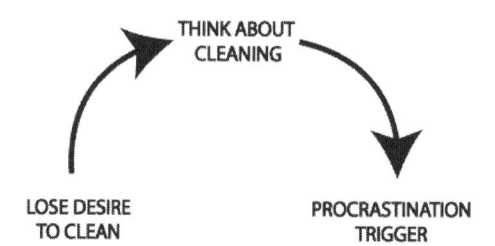

The procrastination cycle starts when you think about cleaning. All it takes is a single thought that you should clean something or do something around the house to trigger the cycle.

This leads to the procrastination trigger.

You start thinking of excuses why you can't clean and allow negative thoughts to invade your thought process. In some cases, the trigger alone is enough to kill all desire to clean.

Procrastination triggers de-motivate you and are the reason you never finish cleaning the house. Let's look at some of the more common triggers of procrastination.

The "I Have To" Mentality

Thinking that you have to get something done makes you feel like you're being forced to do something you don't want to do. The natural response to being forced to do something is to fight doing it.

When this battle is fought internally, you're defeating yourself over and over again without realizing what you're doing. You tell yourself that you *have to* get the house cleaned, which elicits a negative emotional response. This leaves you feeling powerless and unwilling to do the job, all because you feel like it *has to* get done.

If you've got a significant other putting pressure on you to get the house clean, the negative "I have to" response is going to be even greater. How dare someone try to force you into a task you don't want to do? It becomes an excuse not to clean, just to spite the other person.

Turn "I have to" into "I want to" or "I will" and you'll now be associating positive emotions with the task or chore at hand.

Now, you're empowering yourself to get the job done while eliminating the negative emotions associated with the task. You're no longer a victim; you're now an active and willing participant in the process. It's going to take some practice to break this habit, but this is the first procrastination trigger you need to eliminate.

Turn cleaning into a choice you're consciously making instead of something you don't want to do that you're being forced into.

Break It Down

Focusing too much on the big picture is another trigger of the procrastination cycle; instead, pick out little tasks you can easily accomplish. Take it one small step at a time.

When you look at the entire big picture of cleaning your house, it's pretty de-motivating. There's so much that needs to be done, you lose sight of the little tasks required to get to the big picture goal of a completely clean house.

As the little victories begin to build up, you'll start feeling good and the tide will turn in your favor. Instead of procrastinating, you'll find yourself wanting to tackle more chores because you're finally starting to gain some ground.

It's all about breaking cleaning down into manageable chunks.

Do one task until you complete it and move on to the next one. *Don't lose sight of the big picture, but don't solely focus on it.* Rome wasn't built in a day. It wasn't cleaned in a day either. Take care not to focus so much on everything that you end up accomplishing nothing.

Taking action, no matter how small the action is, breaks the procrastination cycle.

Once you've broken the cycle, it's a matter of continuing to achieve small goals that move you in the direction of the greater goal. Stack enough little victories up and you'll end up winning the big game. Your house will be clean and you'll know you're going to be able to keep it that way.

Should Have, Could Have

I could have done better.
I should have done something about this mess a long time ago.

The fact is, you didn't.
Don't dwell on it or you run the risk of triggering the procrastination cycle.
"*Should have, could have*" thinking places a lot of pressure on you to be perfect all the time. You're constantly going to second guess your actions and wonder whether you're making the right choices now. By living in the past, you're dooming yourself to make the same mistakes you've already made.
Stop feeling guilty and blaming yourself for what you should and could have done and starting living in the moment.
You can't change the past, but the future is wide open.
The idea here is to focus on the future, which is the only thing you can change. You will feel better once you start cleaning and getting stuff done. You won't feel better if you sit around and dwell on the past so much that nothing gets done.

Start thinking about the future and what you can do now to work toward where you want to be in the future. Stop living in a past that can't be changed—that is, unless you have a time machine. Then, by all means, go back to the past and kick yourself in the butt for not starting sooner.

Enjoy It, Don't Destroy It

Stop thinking negatively about cleaning and stop destroying the image you have of the tasks required to clean your home. Constantly thinking of how much you hate something throws up red flags in your brain and sets the procrastination cycle in motion.

When you hate something, you can think of all kinds or reasons you can't do it.

It's a lot easier to find time to do something you enjoy.

Reward yourself for getting the job done. By associating rewards with the act of cleaning, you're tricking your mind into making cleaning a positive act instead of a negative one. You'll find yourself looking forward to cleaning time instead of dreading it and wanting to avoid it at all costs.

Another way you can make cleaning a positive experience is to create a playlist of songs you love that you only listen to while cleaning. You'll find yourself looking forward to the time of day you get to listen to your favorite songs instead of dreading the time of day you have to clean.

Create an environment conducive to cleaning that you actually enjoy. This will create a cycle of productivity instead of triggering the procrastination cycle.

Make It Important To You

Why do you clean the house?

If it's because you're worried about what others are going to think, you're doing it for the wrong reason. Doing something because you think others are going to condemn you for not doing it is a good way to build resentment and become an angry person, both on the inside and out.

Instead of cleaning because of what others are going to think if you don't, do it because it's important to you.

There aren't too many people who are actually happy living in a dirty home. If you're one of those people, more power to you. If you're unhappy, then cleaning needs to become something you're doing because you'll be happier living in a clean home. Tell yourself, *"Cleaning is important to me. I'm going to start cleaning right away because I want a clean house."* It might feel forced at first, but if you tell yourself something enough times, you're going to start believing it.

Positive thinking turns into positive cleaning.

Step 2: Go Deep.

Figure 17: If your house looks like this, it's time to get to work.

The second step in the CGM Method is called "Go Deep" for good reason. This is the step in which you *deep clean* your home.

You've made the commitment to keep your home clean and have built up the willpower to stop procrastinating and get to it.

Now comes the hard part.

This is by far the most difficult and time-consuming step in the process. *You're going to have to go through your home and methodically clean it bit by dirty bit.*

If you're like I used to be, you've let things slide for a long time and the mess is getting pretty bad. So bad, in fact, you look around and don't know where to start. I'm going to let you in on a little secret here.

It doesn't matter where you start.

You can start with the dishes piled in the sink. You can start with the piles of laundry in the bedroom. You can start with the clutter built up all over every flat surface in the house. You can start with the carpet or the windows or the garage.

It doesn't matter.

All that matters is you start. And once you start, don't stop.

Don't let the procrastination cycle kick in again and slow you down. Be stubborn. Don't give an inch. Don't allow yourself to find reasons not to clean. Every free minute you have needs to be dedicated to the deep cleaning process.

Depending on just how bad things have gotten, this process could take days, it could take weeks, or it could take months.

No matter how long it takes, don't stop until you've completely finished the deep cleaning process.

I don't mean you have to spend every second of every day cleaning. I recognize you still have a life to live. What I do mean is you need to set aside time *every day* to clean and hold yourself to it. Don't let yourself procrastinate. Catching up on the latest season of the newest Housewives show isn't as important as getting your house clean.

You'll have time for TV later. What matters now is getting through the deep cleaning process.

IMPORTANT TIP

At some point, you're going to look at the mess and start thinking about calling in a housecleaning service to do the deep cleaning step of the CGM cleaning process. I don't recommend you do this unless you have the money to keep paying someone to clean your house. Depending on where you live, it's going to cost anywhere from $50 an hour to $200 an hour to have a maid or two come in and do the cleaning for you. If you have a big mess, it can cost thousands of dollars and take multiple days of cleaning to complete the deep cleaning.

The hourly rate only includes basic cleaning services. Carpet treatment and chemical cleaning costs extra. Furniture cleaning is extra. Window and screen cleaning is extra. So are blinds. The list goes on and on. The costs can really add up fast.

That said, the cost isn't the real reason I don't recommend paying someone to do your deep cleaning.

Part of the process of learning how to clean is doing the deep cleaning yourself and seeing how much work it is to clean your house when you let things get out of control. If you pay to have someone else do it, you're bailing yourself out and will be more likely to let things slide again.

What Is "Deep Cleaning?"

First, we need to define deep cleaning.

I define it as cleaning your home from one end to the other. Everything gets cleaned, top to bottom. Dirt and grime get scrubbed away and you take whatever steps you have to take in order to return your home to as close to new as you can get it.

Deep cleaning renews your home and leaves it smelling and looking fresh and clean.

Looking around you and seeing what needs to be deep-cleaned may evoke feelings of despair. Stop feeling sorry for yourself and knock it off. Remember the section on procrastination triggers? You're not going to let yourself think like that anymore. I'm going to walk you step-by-step through the process of deep cleaning your home.

It's hard, but not as hard as you might think.

We're going to take one room at a time, clean it, then move on to the next room. The key to finishing Step 2 is this: Once you've cleaned a room, you have to keep it clean. Don't let it slide while you're working on other rooms or you devolve into a never-ending cycle of deep cleaning.

Break It Down

Take large cleaning tasks and break them down into smaller, more manageable chunks.

Cleaning the house can be broken down into cleaning each room. Say you choose to clean the kitchen first. This can also be broken down into smaller tasks that are more manageable. When you start looking at each task, you start to see items you can complete.

A dirty room, if left dirty for long enough can become a monster to clean if you look at cleaning the room as a single task. If you break it down into cleaning sections of the room, it becomes much easier.

Create a checklist of the items that need to be cleaned.

A checklist for the kitchen might look something like this:

- ☐ Cabinets.
- ☐ Countertops.
- ☐ Floors.
- ☐ Microwave.
- ☐ Oven.
- ☐ Refrigerator.
- ☐ Sink.
- ☐ Table.
- ☐ Toaster.

Now, take the checklist you have and break it down into manageable cleaning tasks for each of the items on the list:

- Cabinets.
    - Declutter cabinets.
    - Clean out drawers.
    - Wash fronts of cabinets.
    - Repaint cabinets (if needed).
    - Clean tops of cabinets.
- Tile countertops.
    - Clear clutter off of countertops.
    - Clean tiles.
    - Clean grout.
    - Seal grout.
- Floors.
    - Mop floors.
    - Reseal floors.
- Microwave.
    - Clean inside of microwave.
    - Clean outside of microwave.
- Stove.
    - Degrease and clean oven.
    - Clean burners.
    - Clean all other surfaces.
    - Clean and degrease hood.
- Refrigerator.
    - Remove all food.
    - Clean the shelves.
    - Disinfect and deodorize.
    - Put food you plan on keeping back into fridge.
    - Throw old food away and clean out containers.

- ☐ Remove ice from the icemaker and disinfect.
- ☐ Clean the outside of the fridge.
- ☐ Sink
  - ☐ Wash and dry any dishes you have left in the sink.
  - ☐ Scrub the sink.
  - ☐ Deodorize and disinfect the drain.
- ☐ Table.
  - ☐ Clear clutter off the table.
  - ☐ Wash the table.
- ☐ Toaster.
  - ☐ Clean inside.
  - ☐ Clean outside.
- ☐ Walls.
  - ☐ Wash walls.
  - ☐ Clean grease from backsplash.
  - ☐ Touch up paint if necessary.

Once you have a list of all the tasks you need to accomplish, it's time to get to work. Take one task at a time, knock it out and check it off the list.

Top to Bottom Saves Time

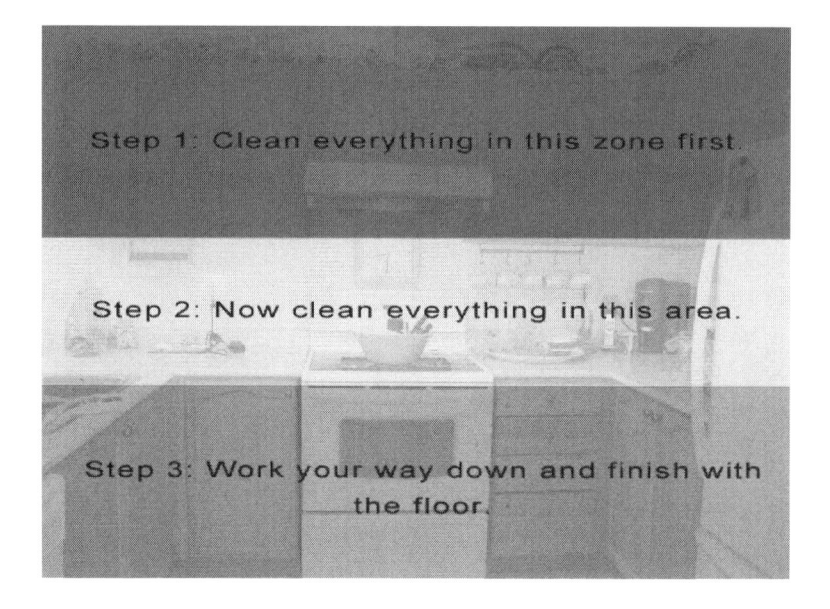

Figure 18: Clean Red-Yellow-Green to avoid re-cleaning items you've already cleaned.

Here's a tip that'll save you a lot of time.

Instead of just randomly choosing cleaning tasks, pick the ones that are at the highest elevations in the room first. The reason for this is simple: gravity.

As you're cleaning the higher areas, dirt and dust is bound to fall on the lower areas. There's no reason to clean the floor first when it's going to get covered with dirt and junk that falls to the ground when you're cleaning the higher areas of the room.

Using the kitchen as an example, clean everything that sits above the countertops before you clean the counters. Next, clean the counters off. Move down to the stuff below the countertops and finish up with the floor. You want to avoid starting off with something low and having to reclean it once you're done cleaning everything that sits above it.

Set Up "Mess Blockers" To Save Time

Figure 19: Stop, no messes allowed.

During the deep cleaning process, try to identify areas where messes tend to form. Then start thinking about "Mess Blockers" you can put in place to prevent the mess from forming in the first place.

"Mess Blockers" are prevention systems designed to keep things organized and clean.

Does clutter always pile up on the flat surface closest to the front hallway? This is a common area for people to set stuff when they walk in the house. Car keys, bills, junk mail, hats and even articles of clothing get added to the ever-growing pile of junk.

Designate certain spaces as "Clear Zones," or places that have to remain clear and free of clutter at all times. Require that coats be hung on a coat rack or put in a hall closet.

Create a hanging system for keys by the door. A few nails hammered into the wall works in a pinch.

Create a system for mail to be processed immediately as it's brought into the house. Junk mail goes right in the trash. Bills and other important pieces of mail are placed in an in-box that's cleared out at the end of each day.

These are just a few "Mess Blockers" you can put in place to make sure messes are stopped dead in their tracks before they have a chance to get out of control. We'll discuss more as we go. The key to these systems is to make sure everyone in the house adheres to them.

A system is only as good as the people using it. You've got to make sure everyone sticks to the plan.

It's not going to be easy at first. In fact, it's going to be downright frustrating when you come home and find your family has been ignoring the new rules all day. You've got to stay firm and make sure they fix the messes they've created. If you get in the habit of doing everything yourself, your family will never learn to follow the rules. *You'll end up stuck in a cycle of cleaning with no help*—and that's not going to accomplish anything other than making you angry.

Let's go room-by-room and cover what you need to clean during the deep cleaning process. Remember, this list is in no particular order. Attack it however you see fit.

You can do the easy stuff first, so you immediately see progress or you can start with the biggest messes and knock them out first in an attempt to make life easier for yourself later on down the road. What matters most is that you get started.

Deep Cleaning the Bathroom

Figure 20: Time to clean the bathroom?

First, the list of tasks:

- **Trash can.**
    - Empty.
    - Disinfect.

- **Cabinets/Medicine cabinet.**
    - Clear out cabinets and drawer.
    - Clean cabinets and drawers.
    - Line cabinets and drawers.
    - Return only the items you need and use to the cabinets and drawers.
    - Wash front of cabinets.
    - Touch up paint, if necessary.
- **Windows.**
    - Take curtains down and wash them.
    - Clean window sills.
    - Wash windows.
- **Floor.**
    - Sweep or vacuum.
    - Mop if hard surface.
    - Clean grout if tile.
    - Seal, if necessary.
- **Light fixture/Fan.**
    - Dust.
    - Replace any burnt out bulbs.
    - Clean fan and fan blades.
- **Shower/Tub**
    - Clean and disinfect.
    - Remove soap scum.
    - Remove mold/mildew and treat surfaces so it doesn't return.
    - Remove calcification from shower head.
    - Remove hard water stains.
    - Apply caulk if necessary.
- **Sink.**

- ☐ Clean and disinfect sink.
- ☐ Remove water stains from faucet.
- ☐ Apply caulk if necessary.
- ☐ **Toilet.**
  - ☐ Clean and disinfect inside and out.
  - ☐ Repair any leaks.
  - ☐ Apply caulk if necessary.
- ☐ **Walls.**
  - ☐ Wash walls.
  - ☐ Touch up paint if necessary.

Since bathroom drawers and cabinets tend to be gathering places for items you don't use or need, let's start there. Before you get started, get 3 large containers. One of the containers is going to be for garbage, one for items you want to keep that don't belong in the bathroom and one for the items you're keeping in the bathroom. Separate everything in the bathroom into one of these 3 containers.

Check the expiration dates on everything as you sort it. If it's outdated, it's time to get rid of it. If you never use it, you shouldn't replace it. You can buy it later on down the road if you end up needing it again. Get rid of any outdated prescription medications you have sitting around.

Once you've sorted everything in the containers, move all 3 containers out of the room. You're going to need room to clean and all the containers will do is get in the way if you leave them in the room. Remember the rule from earlier—clean from the top down.

Wrap a microfiber cloth around the end of a broomstick and use it to clean any cobwebs from the corners of the room. Take the grate off the fan and clean inside it. Dust off the blades.

Clean the light fixtures and replace any missing bulbs. Now's a good time to replace old bulbs with new energy efficient bulbs.

Clean the tops of the cabinets first. Next, clean inside them.

Return the items you plan on keeping in the bathroom to the cabinets. Instead of returning your items to bare cabinets, lay down a layer of shiny paper. I use wrapping paper that's left over from Christmas. Next time you need to clean out your drawers and cabinets all you have to do is pull out the old paper and replace it with new paper. This will save you time the next time you need to clean your drawers.

Designate a place for everything. Nothing should be left sitting on the counters other than a soap dish and your toothbrush holder.

Wipe the outside of the cabinets down last and touch up the paint if you need to.

IMPORTANT TIP

This is your first opportunity to set up a "Mess Blocker."

By designating a place for each item you return to your bathroom, you're going to know exactly where everything needs to go. If you or your family members will have trouble remembering the places items need to be returned to, write the name of each of the items on a piece of masking tape and stick the tape to the designated area until you're used to the item's new home.

Once you're done using an item, return it to its designated spot. Nothing should be left sitting out; everything needs to go "home" once it's no longer in use. This will prevent clutter from building up as you take items out and leave them sitting on the countertops.

Take down any curtains you have in the bathroom and wash them. If they're machine washable, throw them in the washer and clean them while you're working on the rest of the room. If they're not machine washable, wash them according to the manufacturer's instructions.

Throw the shower curtain in the washing machine as well. You'll be able to wash away the soap scum and it's much easier than trying to scrub the curtain clean.

Wash the bathroom window(s) on the inside. Don't worry about the outside. You can clean all of the outside windows in one sweep later instead of going in and out while cleaning each room.

Clean off the window sill. Use a paint brush to clean out the inside of the runners.

Wash the walls and touch up the paint if there are areas with damage. Now would be a good time to fix that towel holder that keeps falling off.

Time to tackle the shower and tub.

Mix one part water with one part distilled white vinegar to create a cleaner capable of removing hard water stains. Wipe down all exposed surfaces with this cleaner.

If there are tough stains or grime, sprinkle baking soda on a sea sponge and scrub the stain or grime away.

Treat mildew and mold with a 50/50 mix of hydrogen peroxide and water. Spray it on the mold and let it sit for 30 minutes before wiping it away. The mold should wipe right off and it won't come back as long as you keep the area it formed in clean and dry.

Treat the shower head for calcification clogging up the nozzles by filling a plastic bag with distilled vinegar. Place the shower head in the plastic bag and tie the bag off so it won't fall off. Let the shower head soak until all of the nozzles are clear.

Check the caulking. If it's damaged, replace it. You don't want water getting where it isn't supposed to go.

Last of all, treat the drain, even if it isn't clogged. Dump half a box of baking soda down the drain. Let it sit for 20 minutes, then pour 2 cups of distilled white vinegar down the drain. Let it bubble up, then wash it down by running warm water down the drain for a couple minutes. Pour boiling water down the drain if you've had trouble with clogged drains in the past.

IMPORTANT TIP

Apply lemon essential oil to the exposed metal areas of the shower door to ease the effects of water spotting.

Next on the agenda is the sink.

Scrub it with natural all-purpose cleaner using generous amounts of cleaner. Use a different sponge to rinse the cleaner away. Wipe down the faucet and use distilled white vinegar on a sponge to get rid of any water spots. Dump half a cup of baking soda down the sink and let it sit for 15 minutes. Follow it up with 1/2 cup of distilled white vinegar. This will help clear any clogs just starting to form.

Check the caulking around the edges of the sink. Lack of caulking around the sink can lead to water leaking down into your cabinets which can lead to rotten wood and mold forming. Repair or replace the caulk, if necessary.

IMPORTANT TIP

Figure 21: Here's a photo of rough pumice. The stones you buy from the store are made of this rock.

There's going to come a time when you go to clean your toilet and there are stains you can't remove no matter how hard you scrub them. These stains are formed by minerals in the water and are nigh on impossible to scrub away with a toilet brush or sponge. I'd go as far as to say they're one of the most stubborn stains you're going to come across while cleaning your home.

Here's a tip I wish I would have known about a long time ago. It would have saved me a lot of time scrubbing away at those difficult water stains to no avail. At one point in my life, I gave up and just let them be. Now, I eliminate them as soon as they start to form with a pumice stone.

Get a pumice stone and use the wet stone to gently rub the stains away.

Pumice stones are made of volcanic rock and can be found in your local beauty supply store or in the beauty supply section of your local department store. Don't scrub too hard and make sure the stone stays wet, as the pumice can scratch and damage the porcelain if used on it while dry. If you're still having trouble getting the stains off, try dipping the stone in baking soda.

Figure 22: The toilet beckons...

Up next, everyone's favorite item to clean: the toilet.

Open the tank and pour a quart of distilled white vinegar into the water. Let it sit while you scrub the outside of the toilet from top-to-bottom. Use a toilet brush to scrub the inside. Once you're done cleaning the toilet, flush it a couple times to wash the distilled white vinegar from the tank.

If the toilet is leaking, chances are it's the flapper valve causing the leak.

When you look into the tank of your toilet, there's a ball that floats up and down as the toilet is flushed. This ball usually has a chain attached to it. The chain is attached to the flapper. The flapper is the rubber piece at the bottom of the toilet that lifts up to let water into the bowl.

It's easy to replace.

Turn off the water supply to your toilet. The valve is located at the back of your toilet where the pipe enters the wall. If there isn't a valve, you're going to have to turn off the water to the house. Flush the toilet a couple times to drain the water from the tank.

Take a picture of how the flapper's hooked up so you'll be able to hook the new one up the same way. Remove the old flapper from the plastic clips and the chain. Take it to your local hardware store and get one just like it. If you're not sure, ask one of the kids wandering the aisles which one you need.

Go home and replace the flapper.

Voila...no more leaky toilet!

Still with me? You're almost done.

The last step is to clean the floors. If you have carpet, clean the carpet and vacuum it. Stubborn stains may require the rental of a steam cleaner. Even then, you may have a tough time getting the stains out.

Now's a good time to replace that carpet with something easier to clean.

Having carpet in the bathroom may keep it a bit warmer, but you're also providing a safe harbor for bacteria and microorganisms to thrive. Replace it with something easy to clean and disinfect like linoleum or tile.

If you already have linoleum or tile, give it a good mopping. You may have to get down and dirty and scrub stubborn stains out of the grout.

Baking soda and a toothbrush work wonders. I've even gone as far as using light grit sandpaper to sand the first layer of grout away to get rid of stubborn stains. Just be careful not to scratch up the tile. Once you're done cleaning the grout, seal it. Sealing the grout will keep the dirt and grime from setting in and will make future cleaning efforts much easier.

That's it. The bathroom is clean.

Depending on the size of your bathroom (and how long it's been since you've cleaned it), this can take anywhere from an hour or two to an entire weekend. Regardless of how long it takes, knock it out a section at a time until you're done.

Once you've finished one bathroom, move on to the rest of the bathrooms in the house. You'll find you get faster as you go because you'll learn little tips and tricks to speed things up. Don't get caught procrastinating. Cleaning all the bathrooms in your house shouldn't take more than a few hours each, unless you've allowed them to get really dirty.

Even then, it probably won't take you more than a weekend to get them clean.

The Kitchen

Figure 23: Messy kitchen.

If you're like me, you spend a lot of time in the kitchen. This is one of the areas of the house where messes tend to build up fast.

Cleaning the kitchen should be a top priority when you start your deep cleaning process because you'll feel good about it when it's done. This make you want to clean more because you'll feel good every time you make a meal in the kitchen and aren't faced with a giant pile of dishes.

Let's first look at the list of tasks you need to get done:

- **Trash can.**
  - Empty.

- ☐ Disinfect.
- ☐ **Light fixture.**
  - ☐ Dust.
  - ☐ Replace any burnt out bulbs.
  - ☐ Clean fan and fan blades.
- ☐ **Counters.**
  - ☐ Clear clutter off counters.
  - ☐ Clean counters.
  - ☐ Don't put anything back on counters other than an item or two left there for decorative purposes.
- ☐ **Cabinets.**
  - ☐ Clear out cabinets and drawer.
  - ☐ Clean cabinets and drawers.
  - ☐ Lay down paper.
  - ☐ Return only the items you need and use.
  - ☐ Wash fronts of cabinets.
- ☐ **Windows.**
  - ☐ Take curtains down and wash them.
  - ☐ Clean window sills.
  - ☐ Wash windows.
- ☐ **Sink.**
  - ☐ Wash and dry dishes.
  - ☐ Clean and disinfect sink.
  - ☐ Remove water stains from faucet.
  - ☐ Apply caulk if necessary.
  - ☐ Deodorize and disinfect the drain/disposal.
- ☐ **Table.**
  - ☐ Clear clutter off table.
  - ☐ Clean table and chairs.

- **Fridge.**
  - Clean outside of fridge.
  - Clear food out.
  - Clean inside fridge.
  - Put only the good food back.
- **Oven.**
  - Clean hood.
  - Wipe outside of oven.
  - Clean grates/burners.
  - Clean inside of oven.
- **Microwave.**
  - Clean inside microwave.
  - Clean outside microwave.
- **Walls.**
  - Wash walls.
  - Touch up paint if necessary.
- **Floor.**
  - Sweep or vacuum.
  - Mop if hard surface.
  - Clean grout if tile.
  - Seal if necessary.

Start with the garbage.

Take it out and disinfect the can(s).

Move on to the light fixtures. Clean them and replace any burnt out bulbs.

Clean out your cabinets and drawers, one at a time. Trash the junk, donate the stuff you don't need and only keep the stuff you actually use. Designate a place for everything. Lay down shiny paper in the drawers and on the cabinet shelves, just like you did in the bathrooms.

The counters come next.

Clear all of the clutter off the countertops. Throw away the stuff you don't need. Donate the stuff that may be useful to others. You don't want anything to go back on the countertops other than a decoration or two. *Keep it minimal*.

A cluttered counter tends to gather even more clutter. Items left on an otherwise clear counter will stick out like a sore thumb and will be hard to ignore.

Avoid tucking items you don't use or need away in cabinets and drawers. I advocate allowing yourself a single junk drawer for stuff you just can't bear to get rid of. When your junk drawer is full, it's time to purge some of the junk. Go through the items in the drawer and throw out the stuff you don't need or don't recognize. Having a little bastion of chaos in an otherwise orderly home helps me maintain my sanity. Just don't allow the mess to spread to other drawers.

We discussed a Mess Blocker for the kitchen countertops in a previous section. Implementing an effective Mess Blocker will allow you to keep counters clear and clean.

The method of cleaning your counters depends on the type of countertops you have. Use the following techniques to clean the various types of countertops:

- **Concrete** should be cleaned with a 1:1 solution of vinegar and water. Clean with a nonabrasive sponge or microfiber cloth.

- **Formica** is cheap and easy to keep clean with soap and warm water. Spills should be wiped up before they have a chance to set.
- **Laminate** counters are inexpensive and easily damaged. Wash them with soap and warm water and steer clear of abrasive cleaners.
- **Granite** is a popular choice in the kitchen. It's a type of rock that is easily damaged by acidic cleaning products like distilled white vinegar. Granite is usually fairly easy to wipe down using a cloth and soapy water. If granite hasn't been sealed properly, it can be porous and stains will set into the granite.
- **Marble** needs to be treated with a stone sealer to keep it from soaking up stains. Wipe up any spills immediately after they happen. Clean marble countertops with Borax and water.
- **Stainless steel** is a fairly new player in the home countertop game. It's been in use for a long time in commercial kitchens because stainless steel counters are easy to wash and keep sanitary. The problem is, they're also hard to keep looking good and to maintain. Wash with warm water and baking soda. Make sure you always dry stainless steel counters thoroughly or you risk permanent discoloration. These counters aren't as stainless as the name implies. Clean with a microfiber cloth to avoid scratching the shiny surface.
- **Tile** is another popular choice for counters. There are more tile countertops than any other

type. Grout should be cleaned with a mixture of baking soda and water. Be sure to completely wash away the baking soda because it can damage the grout if left on for too long. Sealing the grout after cleaning it will make it much easier to clean later on down the road. Just make sure you don't seal stains into the grout.
- **Wood** used to be a popular option for countertops, but has fallen out of favor in recent years. It's easily damaged by water and stains can set into it if spills aren't cleaned up right away. A 1:1 mixture of baking soda to water can be used to clean wood countertops. Wipe your counters with linseed oil after they dry to protect them from the effects of water. Keeping wood countertops in good shape is an uphill battle.

Once you've scrubbed your counters clean, keep them that way. Scrub up any messes or spills immediately, before they have the chance to become nasty stains. Fresh spills take seconds to clean. Stains take minutes or even hours—*if you can get them clean at all*.

Keep counters clear of all but a few aesthetic items. It's up to you whether you want to keep your blender and toaster on the counter, but if you do make sure there's a designated spot for them. I prefer keeping mine tucked away in a cabinet out of sight.

Wash the windows on the inside. You can clean the outside windows all at once later. Take down any curtains and wash them. Clean inside the runners and wipe off the windowsills.

Figure 24: Always run the water when you're running your disposal.

Clean the sink next. Follow the instructions from the bathroom section to clean the sink, with one additional step. Take a whole lemon and drop it into the side of the sink with the garbage disposal. Use the disposal to grind it up. This will eliminate any nasty smells you have coming from the disposal.

Figure 25: Keep your table clear of clutter and it'll be easier to clean.

Declutter your kitchen table.

Nothing should be left on the table except for a centerpiece and maybe some placemats. Find a home for everything else or toss it out. Storing stuff on the table makes your kitchen look cluttered and dirty.

Wipe the table clean with warm soapy water.

IMPORTANT TIP

You may find there's a sticky residue on your wood table that's difficult to wipe off with soapy water. This residue is made up of dirt and grime mixed in with worn-out varnish. It can't be removed with soapy water.

To remove it, create a 1:1 mixture of water and distilled white vinegar and use it to wipe the table down. The acid in the vinegar will lift up the worn out varnish. Just don't scrub too hard. You can leave permanent streaks on the surface of the table.

Figure 26: Oh boy, this is going to take a while.

Time to tackle the appliance that never takes a break—your fridge.

Take all of the food out of the freezer first.

Throw out any food that's old or outdated. Set the rest in a large ice chese. Let the freezer sit open while you clean out the fridge so it'll have time to defrost.

Clear out the fridge and toss out all the science experiments you've been growing in the back. Fridges are a funny thing. Once food makes its way to the back of the fridge, it's often left there for weeks (or even months) on end. By the time you find it again, it's taken on a life of its own, with all sorts of crazy stuff growing on it or in it.

You're going to have to make a choice when it comes to cleaning out the food in your fridge. You can do things the easy way and throw all the old food, containers and all, in a garbage bag and throw it out, or you can toss just the food in a garbage bag and clean the containers out one at a time. If you want to save your Tupperware and choose the latter, I hope you have a strong stomach. Things can get pretty bad in the back of the fridge.

Place the food items you plan on keeping in the ice chest with the items from the freezer. The frozen items from the freezer will help keep the items from the fridge cool.

Once you've got all the food out of the fridge, it's time to clean the inside. Wipe up any spills and clean the inside with a 1:1 mixture of baking soda and warm water. Make sure you clean the door seals and any cracks that may be harboring crumbs and food particles.

Once your fridge is clean, put the food back.

Clean the outside of the fridge next. Use vinegar and water to clean stainless steel refrigerators and warm, soapy water for all other types. Wipe down the front, sides and the top. Dust and vacuum the back of the fridge. Make sure you clean the coils, but be careful not to damage them. Roll the fridge out and clean underneath it.

IMPORTANT TIP

Glass shelves and drawers shouldn't be cleaned with warm soapy water while they're cold.

Trust me on this one. I've got a large crack running through one of my shelves because I got impatient and tried to clean a shelf before it had a chance to reach room temperature.

IMPORTANT TIP

Fridge gunk can be hard to wipe away.
Create a paste using baking soda and water. Apply the paste to the gunk and let it sit for 20 minutes. The gunk should wipe right off. For large areas of build-up, you may have to apply the paste a few times.

IMPORTANT TIP

A fridge that's been neglected for a long time can take on a smell that's tough to get rid of.
Mix baking soda and coffee grounds in a tray and leave the tray sitting in the fridge for a few days. This will eventually get rid of the smell. Avoid further problems with bad smells by cutting the top off of a box of baking soda and leaving it in the door of the fridge.

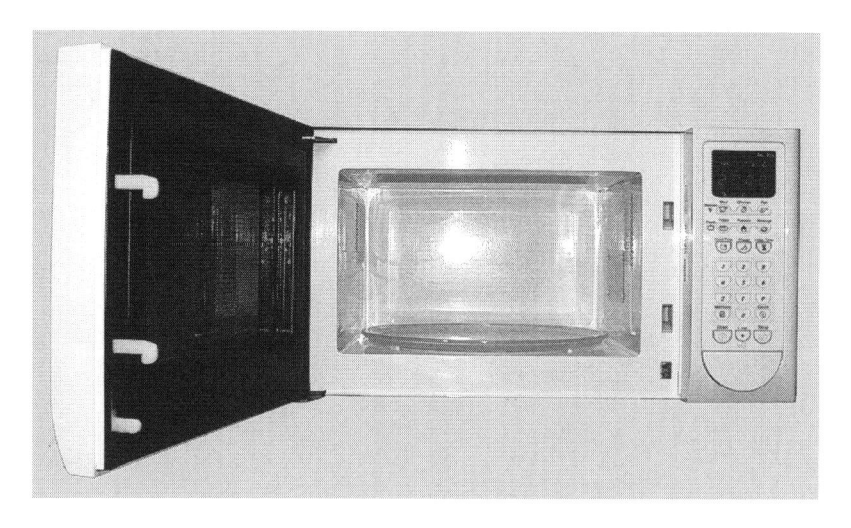

Figure 27: This is what your microwave should look like after every use. Spotless.

Time to tackle the microwave, which should be a breeze because you've been wiping it down after every use. You have been wiping it down, haven't you? OK, maybe the microwave isn't going to be so easy, but here's a trick you can use to speed up the process.

Take a glass bowl and fill it with a cup of water with the juice of two lemons squeezed into it. Place the bowl in the microwave and heat it until the water's boiling. Let it boil for around 30 seconds. The previously rock-solid gunk in your microwave should just wipe away. If not, bring the lemon water to a boil again and let it boil for a little longer this time.

Clean the inside and move on to the outside.

Figure 28: Give your stove a good deep-cleaning and leave it looking like this.

If you're anything like me, you saved the oven for last. The baked on grease and food isn't going to be easy to get off, but with a little work, you can get rid of most of it.

Make a paste by adding baking soda to water until it's a thick consistency. If you want it to smell good, add a few drops of your favorite essential oil to the paste. Apply a thin coating of the paste to the inside of your oven. If your stovetop is in bad shape too, apply the paste to that as well.

Let it sit overnight.

In the morning, get a bucket of soapy water and use a sea sponge to remove the grime. It should come right off. For stubborn cooked-on food, try wiping it off with distilled white vinegar.

IMPORTANT TIP

Here's a simple tip most people don't think of.

I know when a friend told me about it, I wanted to slap myself on the forehead and say DOH! You don't have to spend hours scrubbing you burners or drip trays. If you can remove them, just take them out and throw them in your dishwasher. Simple and quick. No scrubbing needed.

Now that's simplicity!

The last step should be cleaning your floors.

Most kitchen floors can be mopped. If yours can be mopped, dry mop it first to get all the loose debris up, then wet mop it to clean the surface. If you have tile, seal the grout once you've cleaned it.

Congrats, you just finished cleaning the kitchen. The hardest room in the house to clean and to keep clean is complete. Now that you've got it in good shape, keep it that way. It's a lot easier than having to deep clean it every time you decided to clean house.

Living Room/Family Room

Figure 29: If your living room looks like this, you're not living minimally.

First, the list:

- **Light fixtures.**
    - Dust.
    - Replace any burnt out bulbs.
    - Clean fan and fan blades.
- **Fireplace.**
    - Clear clutter off mantle.
    - Keep decorations minimal.
    - Clean inside of fireplace.
- **Furniture.**
    - Clean sofa.
    - Clean coffee table.

- ☐ Clean chairs.
- ☐ **Windows.**
  - ☐ Take curtains down and wash them.
  - ☐ Clean window sills.
  - ☐ Wash windows.
  - ☐ Clean blinds.
- ☐ **TV.**
  - ☐ Clean TV.
  - ☐ Sort wires behind TV.
- ☐ **Walls.**
  - ☐ Wash walls.
  - ☐ Touch up paint if necessary.
- ☐ **Floor.**
  - ☐ Sweep or vacuum.
  - ☐ Mop if hard surface.
  - ☐ Clean grout if tile.
  - ☐ Seal if necessary.

Start with the light fixtures.

Clean off your ceiling fan blades. You'd think the dirt and dust would blow off while the fan spins, but it doesn't. You'll be amazed by how much dirt builds up on top of the blades.

Replace any burnt out bulbs.

Clean your windows and curtains next.

Nothing new here. This has already been covered in previous sections.

Figure 31: Clean the outside yourself, but leave cleaning the flue to the pros.

Your fireplace is one area I don't recommend you try to clean yourself—at least not on the inside. Clear all the clutter off the mantle and take down those stockings you've had up since Christmas. Wipe the mantle down and exercise control when you begin putting stuff back up. Only put back a decorative item or two. You want it to look clean and clear, not cluttered and messy.

You can clear the soot and ashes from the hearth, but call in a professional to clean the creosote from the chimney and flue unless you know what you're doing. This tar-like substance builds up and can be a fire hazard if it isn't cleaned regularly.

Dust the hearth and wipe the outside of the fireplace down with a 1:1 vinegar to water solution. Take extra care to clean off any soot or dust that's built up.

IMPORTANT TIP

The Clean Green Minimal cleaning method advocates that you always use natural cleaners. When it comes to cleaning your fireplace, this is especially important.

A lot of commercial cleaners are flammable and should never be used inside the fireplace. Stick with baking soda or distilled white vinegar and avoid the risk of leaving a residue behind that can cause a fire.

Furniture time!

We've already covered how to clean and seal wood furniture, so I'm not going to go over it again. Let's take a look at how you can naturally remove stains from fabric.

The following techniques have all proven effective:

- **Create a mixture of 3 parts baking soda to 1 part club soda.** Rub the liquid into the stain and let it sit for 5 minutes. Wipe the area that's stained down. Most stains will come right out.
- **Denatured alcohol works well for cleaning suede.**
- **Microfiber can usually be cleaned just by wiping it down with warm water.** If that doesn't work, try a baby wipe.
- **Distilled white vinegar and water can be used to remove pee stains from most fabrics.** Sprinkle baking soda on the wet spot to get rid of the smell.

Don't forget to clean beneath your furniture.

All kinds of junk can build up underneath your sofa. I constantly find toys and loose change under my sofa.

Figure 32: Be glad you don't have this many TVs to clean.

Your TV accumulates an incredible amount of dust.

Use a can of compressed air to blow excess dust out of the cracks and crevices of your TV. Shoot the air in any holes you find to blow excess dust out. Be prepared to make a mess. Hope you didn't vacuum before you started cleaning your TV. You'll be doing it again once you're done with this step.

Dust the top of your TV and wipe down the screen.

Now comes the fun part. Pull your TV stand out and sort the wires out. It's crazy how the wires seem to tie themselves in knots after sitting untouched for months. Sort out the mess and tie up any loose wire with zip ties.

Wash the walls and touch up the paint where necessary.

Figure 33: Light-colored carpet looks great when it's new, but kids and pets can take care of that in a jiffy.

The last step is to clean the floors.

Wash or dry mop wood floors. If you have carpet, the level of cleaning required depends on what kind of shape the carpet is in. You might be able to get away with sprinkling baking soda around on the carpet and letting it sit overnight before vacuuming it. Take your time vacuuming the carpet and make sure you pass over each area a couple times.

Carpet that's in really bad shape may need to be steam cleaned. You can rent a cleaner from some grocery stores or you can pay to have it done by a professional. Follow the instructions on the cleaner.

A solution of white vinegar and water can be used to lift tough stains. Apply it and let it dry, then scrub the spot with warm soapy water. The vinegar may lift the stain out of the carpet.

Bedroom(s)

Figure 34: Make the bed and your room will look 200% cleaner.

Here's the list of stuff you need to get done in the bedroom:

- **Light fixtures.**
    - Dust.
    - Replace any burnt out bulbs.
    - Clean fan and fan blades.
- **Windows.**
    - Take curtains down and wash them.
    - Clean window sills.
    - Wash windows.
    - Clean blinds.

- **TV.**
    - Clean TV.
    - Sort wires behind TV.
- **Furniture.**
    - Clean beds.
    - Wash bedding.
    - Clean and declutter dressers and nightstands.
- **Closet.**
    - Clean closet out.
    - Get rid of clothes that don't fit or you don't wear.
- **Walls.**
    - Wash walls.
    - Touch up paint if necessary.
- **Floor.**
    - Vacuum.

Take care of the light fixtures first.

You know the routine.

Take care of the windows next. You know what to do here, too.

The TV's next. You've done it before.

Figure 35: When it comes to decorations, think minimal. It's easier to clean when you only have a handful of items you need to work around.

There are a couple new pieces of furniture in the bedroom that you haven't had to clean yet.

The dressers and nightstands need to be decluttered and dusted. Keep decorations and items left on the dressers and nightstands to the bare minimum of what you need. I have a decoration or two on my dressers and an alarm clock on my nightstand—that's it. It helps me see when something's out of place.

Clear the drawers out one at a time.

Get rid of all the junk you've accumulated over the years. Sort all of the clothes you pulled from the dressers and get rid of the stuff you haven't been able to fit into since high school. Get rid of the stuff that's outdated, too. If you don't already do so, designate drawers for each article of clothing. Fold the clothes and put them back in the drawers.

Do the same thing with the clothes and junk in your closets. Get rid of everything you don't need and neatly fold and hang the rest.

IMPORTANT TIP

Here's another opportunity to create a Mess Buster.

Sort all dirty laundry into piles and move it to the laundry room, so it's not cluttering up your room.

Set up a system for storage of dirty clothes. A couple clothes hampers (one for whites and one for brights) works well. Insist the pockets on all clothes are cleaned out *before* they're put in the hamper. This will save you time when you're doing the laundry.

Don't allow family members to get away with tossing clothes on the floor or in the wrong hamper. Make them fix their mistakes until they get used to the new system.

Better yet, train family members to do their own laundry. That'll save you a lot of time in the long run. I'm of the opinion anyone in the house over 10 years of age should be doing their own laundry. You'll have to supervise things closely at first, but it's worth it when your kids are able to do their own laundry without your help a month or two down the road.

Remove the sheets from the bed and put them in the wash. If your washer can handle quilts and blankets, wash them as well. If not, take them to the Laundromat and wash them.

Put the clean bedding back on the bed and you're good to go.

Clean the walls. Vacuum the floor and remove any visible stains.

The Laundry Room

This list is short, but it can be deceptively difficult to complete and stay on top of:

- **Do laundry.**
    - Clean it.
    - Sort it.
- **Clean the laundry room.**

Figure 36: Where's this place at?

You're on the home stretch now. You've finished all the rooms in the house and are ready to tackle the mountains of laundry you have piled up.

IMPORTANT TIP

If your laundry pile puts Mount Rushmore to shame, it's going to take a loooooooong time to do your laundry at home. You can do it; you're just going to have to be diligent about it.

What if I told you there's a way you could get it all done in a couple hours, but it would cost you a hundred bucks or so? If you want to know, send me a check for at least a hundred bucks and I'll e-mail you the technique.

Figure 37: Take your clothes to the Laundromat and finish your laundry in record time.

Just kidding.

It's still going to cost you, but you're not going to have to pay me. You're going to have to pay the Laundromat. People with washing machines tend to avoid the Laundromat like the plague. This is one of the few times where using the Laundromat can really save you time. Find a Laundromat that isn't busy and do multiple loads at once.

Wash them, dry them and you're done with all of your laundry in a fraction of the time it would have taken to do at home.

Figure 38: Simple laundry room.

Clean your laundry room.

Clear off the cabinets and the top of the washer and dryer. Clean out your drawers and line them with paper. Wash the sink.

Run an empty load through your washer with a cup of distilled white vinegar thrown in to clear out soap scum. Clean your lint traps and clear the lint from the dryer vent.

Clean the floor.

The laundry room is complete. Let out a deep sigh of relief.

Outside

Figure 39: This is a neglected home.

If you've been neglecting the outside areas of your home for a long time, it might be best to pay a landscaper to get things in order. Or you can make your husband and kids get out there and get to work while you're cleaning the inside.

You might also need to pay to have it painted. If your paint is peeling off in sheets and the wood is starting to crack and dry out, you're going to need to do something about it. It can get expensive, but investing money in maintaining your house costs less than paying for expensive repairs down the road.

Here's what needs to be done:

- ☐ **Clean the outside of the house.**
    - ☐ Pressure wash walls.
    - ☐ Wash windows.
    - ☐ Paint window frames.
- ☐ **Lawn and garden.**
    - ☐ Mow lawns.
    - ☐ Do yard work.
    - ☐ Repair/replace broken sprinklers.
- ☐ **Sidewalks/Driveway.**
    - ☐ Pressure wash sidewalks and driveway.

You're going to need to rent a pressure washer to wash your sidewalks, driveway and the outside of your house. Notice I said rent. Unless you want to invest thousands of dollars on a professional model of your own, *you're better off renting a good pressure washer than you are buying a cheap one*. The cheap ones run you around a hundred bucks. In my experience they don't work well and break after a few uses. Spend a few bucks and rent a good one or invest a thousand or more to buy a good one.

You get what you pay for when it comes to pressure washers. Learn from my mistakes!

Rent a pressure washer for a day and clean the entire outside of your house, along with your driveway and any other concrete you have. You can also use it to spray your screens clean.

Just don't try to wash your car with it. Learn from my mistakes here too. A pressure washer placed too close to a car can make small dents you don't notice until the sun hits it just right.

Figure 40: Get to work. The windows aren't going to wash themselves.

Wash all of the outside windows in one sweep.

If you live in a two-story house, you can either climb a ladder and wash the 2nd-story windows or you can pay a pro. Use white distilled vinegar mixed with water for the cleaning and wipe it dry with a microfiber cloth. The vinegar will help prevent streaking.

Figure 41: Nice lawn. How come my lawn never looks like this?

Mow your lawns.

Just for the record, I absolutely hate mowing lawns and avoid it at all costs. So does everyone else in my household. I found a neighborhood kid who's willing to do it for $20 a month. He comes once a week and mows the front and back. He's happy, I'm happy. My hubby and kids are happy.

Finish up any yard work you've been neglecting.

Check your sprinkler system for any broken or missing sprinkler heads and replace them. You might unknowingly be wasting a lot of water if you have a few missing sprinkler heads. They're easy to replace. Unscrew the broken head and take it to your local hardware store. Get one just like the one you have in your hand, bring it home and screw it into place.

The Garage

Figure 42: Your garage?

On to the last area you need to clean: your garage.

The garage should be the last area you clean because you're probably going to end up moving items you're not sure you want to keep to the garage during previous steps.

It's time to sort through those items with a critical eye. Ask yourself if you really need each item. If you're not sure, ask yourself when you're going to use it again. If the answer to the first question is no or the second question is you don't know, you need to get rid of the item. You can throw it away, donate it or have a garage sale to get rid of a bunch of items at once.

Designate a place for everything.

Your garage should be as neat and orderly as the rest of your house. Once you've sorted and organized everything, sweep the floors. If you're really feeling industrious, you can move everything out of the garage and pressure wash the concrete and seal it.

Treat the garage the same way you did the drawers and cabinets in your house. You need to designate a place for everything and keep everything in its place. Tools, brooms, fishing poles, etc. Every item you're storing in your garage should have a home. If you bring something new in, designate a place for it.

Pat Yourself On the Back.

Once you've completed Step 2 and have given your home a thorough deep cleaning, give yourself a good pat on the back. Most people don't make it through this step. They stop and start in fits and never make it through to the easy part. You're the exception to the rule.

Congratulations!

It's been a lot of work, but I've got some good news for you.

As long as you don't let things slip back into disarray, you'll never have to do this much work again. It's a lot easier to maintain things than it is to deep clean them.

You may have rooms in your house that I didn't cover in this section. *You've now got the skills you need to clean any room.* The steps are simple: Declutter and deep clean from the top to the bottom.

Rinse and repeat.

Step 3: Maintain.

Now for the "easy" part.

Well, at least easier than deep cleaning. Now that you've got your home clean, you're going to need to keep it that way.

Step 3 is the Maintain step. This is the step where you keep everything clean. This step should be done in a continuous cycle with Step 4, the Spring Cleaning step.

Maintaining means *never* letting things get out of control again. You've got to get in the habit of cleaning messes when they're made—or at least when you notice them—and not ignoring them until the disaster in your house reaches critical mass. You've got to stop what you're doing and clean things up immediately whenever you notice a mess.

No more putting off cleaning until you have time. *The time is now*. When you go to bed at the end of the day, the house should be as clean as it was when you woke up.

You can now keep your house clean in around a half hour a day.

Yes, I am serious. That's all it's going to take.

Here's what you have to do.

When you get up in the morning and take off your pajamas, throw them in the dirty clothes hampers you have set up instead of onto the floor. The same thing needs to happen every time you change your clothes. Pockets get cleaned out and the clothes get sorted into the correct hamper.

As you're getting ready for your day, put everything you get out away as soon as you're done with it. Take a bath or shower and give the tub or shower a quick wipe-down when you're done. Same thing goes for the sink after you brush your teeth and finish primping.

Clean as you go while making breakfast.

Anything you don't clean while making breakfast should be cleaned up immediately after you're done eating. Wipe anything you spill up immediately. Don't leave dishes piled in the sink. Wipe them down and put them in the dishwasher. If you don't have a full load, leave the dishes sitting in the dishwasher until you do. Wipe the table clean. Do the same thing with all of your meals throughout the day.

As you go about your daily business, be diligent about watching for messes starting to form or stuff that's out of place. It's going to take a conscious effort at first because you're going to have to form the habit of seeing and taking care of messes to replace your old habit of ignoring them until they reach critical mass. Once you've done it for a while, noticing messes is going to become second nature.

Take a minute or two to clean the little messes up when you notice something isn't right. You can stop big messes dead in their tracks by taking care of the little messes you see instead of ignoring them.

In order to keep things clean in a minimal amount of time, you're going to need to keep things minimal. Keep the stuff you have sitting out to a bare minimum. Having only a few decorations doesn't just make things easier on you; it makes your house appear cleaner.

If you have thousands of knick-knacks spread throughout your home, dusting alone is going to take hours as you try to work your way around each fragile piece.

On the other hand, if all flat spaces are relatively clear and you only have a few items to work your way around, the time required to dust is kept to a bare minimum. *This is where minimalism really comes into its own in regard to keeping your house clean.*

It's up to you to decide just how minimal you want to be. Just remember, the less stuff you own, the less stuff you have that needs to be cleaned and the faster you'll get your cleaning tasks done and be able to move on to the stuff you really enjoy.

Tasks like dusting and vacuuming don't need to be done every day. Some cleaning tasks only need to be done once a week or even once every couple of weeks.

Schedule them for once or twice a week. Set a regular day time for these tasks and make sure they get done on that day. Don't let these tasks slide for weeks on end or you'll end up having to go back to the deep cleaning stage.

Tips To Help Keep the House Clean

It's all too easy to backslide and let things get out of control again.

The best advice I can give is to never go more than 2 days without cleaning. If you slip or are too busy one day, you need to go out of your way the next day to make sure you clean house.

Here are some tips you can use to speed up the process:

- **Do a clean sweep of the house every night.** Yes, that includes your kid's rooms. Make them clean up any messes they've made while you pick up the rest of the house.
- **Institute a "Nothing Left on the Floors" policy.** Nothing other than the furniture should be touching the floor at the end of the day.
- **When you bring new stuff into the house, throw old stuff out.** This will prevent clutter from building up.
- **When it comes time to clean, ignore phone calls until you're done.** There isn't much that can't wait. Don't answer the phone or stop to watch TV until you're done cleaning.
- **Do laundry as soon as you have a load ready.** Don't let it build up into multiple loads. Do it as you get to one load instead of waiting until you have 10 loads laying around.
- **Wipe down toilets and sinks once every couple of days.**

- **Carry cleaning supplies with you and go on a mission to find messes during your clean sweep.** That way, if you do find something, you can clean it right away without having to run all over the house looking for supplies.
- **Don't put off until tomorrow what you can do today.** Tomorrow never comes. Today is the time to clean things you see that need to be done.

Put Your Family To Work

Enlist the help of every single person living in the house that's capable of walking around and making a mess.

If they're old enough to make a mess, they're old enough to help clean it. It's going to feel like mission impossible at first. You're going to have to tell your kids the same thing over and over again until you feel like you're talking to a brick wall. You're going to feel the same way about your husband.

You might even think about buying all of them a one-way plane ticket out of the country.

Don't fret.

Eventually they'll all get tired of listening to you and start doing things your way. Just don't give in and do the cleaning for them. If they think you're going to break down and do the cleaning yourself, they're going to try to wait you out.

Be consistent, even when you feel things are hopeless.

Kids as young as 2 or 3 can be taught to pick up after themselves.

Create a Mess Blocker rule that states toys have to be put away before other toys can be brought out. The toughest part is going to be enforcing the rule until it becomes a habit. Once it's a habit, it's a breeze.

I had my daughter doing her own laundry by the time she was 6 years old. She came in and watched me do it enough times that she learned how to do it. I sat and watched over her shoulder until she was 7 and she's been doing it all on her own ever since. People are shocked when

I tell them how old she was when I had her start doing her own laundry. What I ask them is what's the worst thing that could happen? It's not like she's going to fall into our front loading washing machine and get stuck in there on a spin cycle.

The natural cleaners we use aren't harsh chemicals that can cause burns. When she does get a little bit on her hands, she knows to wash it off. The worst thing that's happened in the years she's been doing her laundry is she dropped the container of laundry detergent one day and we had to sweep and vacuum it up.

It took about an hour to clean. That's a price I'm willing to pay for years of not having to do her laundry.

Older kids can be enlisted to help out with a lot of the daily chores. Cleaning the dishes and the table after meals are both good tasks to hand off to the kids. My kids also dust, do yard work, clean their bathroom and their rooms.

Believe it or not, husbands can be enlisted to help, too. They're not going to open to it at first, but you've got to be firm and at the *very least* demand they don't make messes.

My entire family helps keep the house clean. I demand that they help.

It wasn't always this way; I used to kill myself trying to do everything on my own. Now, I've got plenty of help. It wasn't easy at first, but I've got everyone in my house trained to work with me instead of against me.

You can do it, too.

Eliminate "Time Vampires"

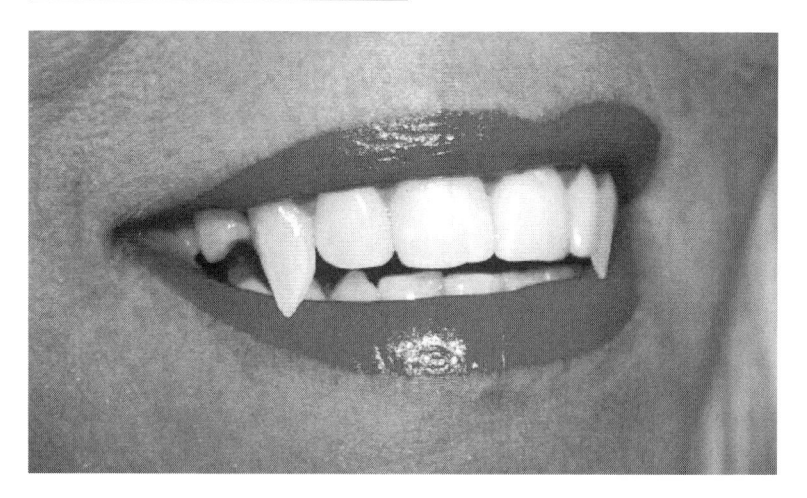

Figure 43: I'm here to drain you of your time.

In my efforts to come up with the fastest, easiest cleaning method, I came across what I like to call "*Time Vampires.*" These Time Vampires suck down time like a vampire drinks blood and cause you to waste time on meaningless tasks that don't help your cleaning efforts one bit. They sap you of time, energy and willpower.

By identifying and eliminating Time Vampires, you can maximize the time you spend cleaning and make every minute spent cleaning count.

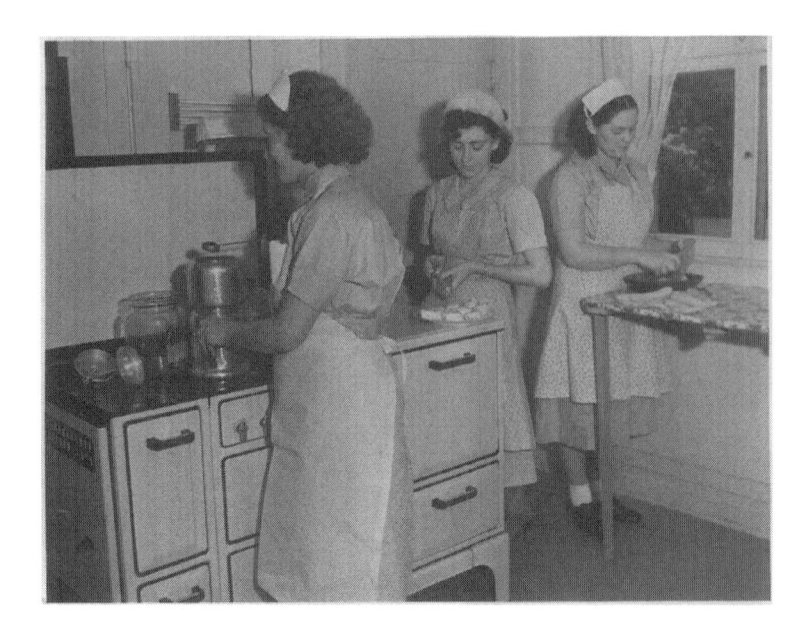

Figure 43: Watch maids at work to learn the secrets of the pros.

You can learn a lot from watching a maid service come in and clean a home. If you have the money, it might be worth paying to have a maid come in one time to clean your home from top to bottom.

Just don't cheat and have them come in for the deep cleaning process. You need to go through that step to get ready for the Maintaining step.

Watch the maid as she works. There's no wasted time.

No running back and forth from room to room to get supplies left in other rooms. All the supplies the maid needs are carried with her in one caddy. Everything she plans on using is kept with her and carried into the next room.

She'll attack a room and keep cleaning until the entire room has been cleaned, then move on to the next room. Cleaning is done one room at a time, not one task at a time.

She won't dust the entire house and then wash all the windows in the house, then vacuum the entire house. A good maid knows it's much faster to clean an entire room before moving on to the next room. Once a room's done, she won't go back into that room.

This is the first Time Vampire you need to eliminate. Bouncing around from room to room. Stay in one room and clean it until the entire room is clean, then move on to the next room.

It's all about efficiency.

There's no wasted time. This is especially true for maids that are working for themselves instead of a company that pays them by the hour. Self-employed maids make more money by being able to clean more houses. They'll work as expediently as they can to get the job done and move on to the next home. Time is money and they learn quickly how to save time without cutting corners.

Here's another Time Vampire professional maids have eliminated: wasted time switching back and forth between cleaning supplies and tools.

I used to wash windows by spraying a section at a time, then wiping it down. I'd spray the section of the window I was washing, then set down the bottle and pick the rag up to wipe the window down. When I started looking at how to speed things up, I figured out that it was faster to spray all the windows in the room and then wipe them clean.

I was pretty proud of my discovery until I watched a maid clean the windows in a room.

What I saw amazed me. It was pure efficiency in action. She held the spray bottle of cleaner in one hand and the cloth in the other. She sprayed a section of window with the bottle in one hand and was already wiping with the other by the time the mist settled on the glass. Both hands were in constant motion: spraying and wiping, wiping and spraying.

I realized then that this technique could be used all over the house.

Unless you have to let your cleaner sit for a while to really soak in, use the spray and wipe technique to speed up your cleaning efforts.

You can really take things to the next level by trying to get everything done in one pass through the room.

Using the kitchen as an example, you could start at the sink, clean it and wipe down the counters within reach. Move down to the fridge, cleaning all the counters and cabinets in your path, then clean the fridge and keep on trucking.

IMPORTANT TIP

I learned something else from watching a maid service clean.

Cleaning needs to be treated like a job.

Schedule a certain time every day for cleaning and stick to it. By setting a schedule, you're making time for cleaning and forcing yourself to consciously decide to clean. You're going to be consciously forcing yourself to decide not to clean on the days you feel like skipping out on your responsibilities.

When it's time to clean, everything else should be left behind. Turn the TV off, put on some music you enjoy and get down to business. Don't stop until you're done. Stick with it and minimize distractions and you'll be done before you know it.

Cleaning tasks seem to drag on forever when you're stopping and starting the task because you're distracted by other stuff. A five minute counter wipe-down can take an hour if you take breaks to watch parts of your favorite TV show, go to the bathroom, play with the kids and answer a phone call you could have ignored.

Once you start cleaning something, it should take an act of God to stop you.

Limit distractions and get the job done faster.

I know this has already been covered in previous sections, but it bears mention again.

Clutter is one of the biggest Time Vampires there is.

Having to sort through piles of junk every time you clean will bring your cleaning to a screeching halt. So will having to clean in and around a bunch of decorations or knick-knacks. Keep the items you have sitting on flat surfaces to a minimum to really cut down the time it takes to clean.

If you have hundreds of items sitting out that you have to move to clean around and beneath them, you're going to spend a lot of time just moving stuff around. You've got to pick up each item to dust and clean the area around it, plus you've got to spend time cleaning the item itself. It may not seem like it, but the time spent doing this adds up quickly. If you have 30 knick-knacks in your house and you spend a minute cleaning each of them, you've just wasted 30 minutes that could have been spent doing something else.

This is time you could be spending doing stuff you actually enjoy. Keep an item or two you really like out and pack up the rest.

Items left sitting out of place take up just as much time. Keep stuff picked up and don't let little items sit around. If you're constantly clearing clutter and putting it in its place, you're not going to spend hours cleaning up clutter every time you decide to clean the counters. The counters will be clear and it'll only take 5 to 10 minutes or so to give them a good wipe-down.

Another big Time Vampire is the tendency to overcomplicate cleaning tasks.

You can get by with only the tools in this book and the green cleaners I've given you recipes for. A general all-purpose green cleaner can be created from baking soda and water or distilled white vinegar and water. This cleaner can be used on most surfaces in the house.

There's no need to spend tons of money on the specialized "green" cleaners sold in the stores. Make your own and save money. You'll also save time because you won't have 20 different bottles spread out across the house you have to sort through to find the cleaner you need. *You'll have a few bottles you can carry around with you that can be used for pretty much everything.*

Here's one last Time Vampire you can eliminate.

When you're making your natural cleaners, mix them up in a big batch.

It'll take you close to the same amount of time to make a large batch as it will a small batch and you won't have to mix up a new batch of cleaner every single time you want to clean.

Step 4: Spring Cleaning

No matter how hard you try, there's always going to be something that slips by.

Maybe it's cleaning the outside walls of the house. Maybe it's your yard work. Maybe it's cleaning the oil spots beneath where you park your car in the garage.

There's always going to be something.

For this reason, a good "spring cleaning" once or twice a year is an absolute necessity.

During spring cleaning, you go through the house with a fine tooth comb and complete the tasks you've been ignoring or neglecting. Some tasks, like pressure washing the house and driveways, only need to be done once or twice a year.

Create a list and consult that list when it comes spring cleaning time. Take a weekend and get all of the tasks on the list done.

Spring cleaning is also a good time to make any necessary repairs on the house. Replace those missing or broken fence boards, patch the cracks in the concrete and replace that tile you broke when you dropped your bowling ball.

You get the point.

By creating a constant cycle of Step 3 and Step 4, you can keep your home clean in the minimal amount of time possible. You need to maintain as much as you can, then use Spring Cleaning to fill in the gaps.

Clean Green Goodbye

That's it. The Clean Green Minimalist Method of cleaning. Not too bad, right?

By combining minimalism and green cleaning techniques, you can clean your home quickly and naturally, and—once you've done the initial deep cleaning—you can keep it clean in less than a half hour a day.

This isn't a pipe dream.

It works. I'm living proof.

So are my ever-growing group of loyal followers. You can clean your home and keep it that way. You just have to make the decision right now to change your life. Do it the safe and easy way—the Clean Green Minimalist way.

Thanks for purchasing (or borrowing) this book. Stay tuned for more Clean Green Minimalism books in the near future.

Now get to cleaning.
Use green cleaners.
Simplify as much as possible.
Don't stop until your house is clean.
Keep it that way.

The previous 5 sentences are CGM cleaning in a nutshell. Come to think of it, I really didn't need to write this book at all. I could just tell people those 5 simple sentences and leave it at that.